THE
SUN'S
EYE

NEW EDITION

West Indian Writing for Young Readers

Compiled by
Anne Walmsley

Cover Illustration:
'Carnival' by Art Derry

Orders: please contact Bookpoint Ltd, 130 Park Drive, Milton Park, Abingdon, Oxon OX14 4SE. Telephone: (44) 01235 827720. Fax: (44) 01235 400454. Email: education@bookpoint co.uk.

Lines are open from 9 a.m. to 5 p.m., Monday to Saturday, with a 24-hour message answering service, You can also order through our website: www.hoddereducation.com

First published 1968
Second edition 1989

First published by Longmans, Green and Co.Ltd
This edition published by Longman Group UK Ltd,
Part of Pearson Education
Published from 2015 by Hodder Education,
An Hachette UK Company
Carmelite House
50 Victoria Embankment
London EC4Y 0DZ
www.hoddereducation.com

20 19
IMP 6

Set in 10/13pt Palatino Roman
Printed and bound by CPI Group (UK) Ltd, Croydon, CRO 4YY

ISBN 978-0-582-76649-5

Illustrations accompanying the poems and stories

We are grateful to the following artists for their illustrations as follows:
Paul Dash for pages 39, 57, 58, 95; Art Derry for pages 3, 10, 52, 74; Errol Lloyd for pages 21, 64, 103; Dennis Ranston for pages 6, 43, 50, 77, 87, 108, 111, 115, Trevor Waugh for pages 16, 17, 19, 37, 62, 63, 68, 98, 99, 119.

Contents

iv

Introduction

For a book prepared in the early '60s still to be in demand in the late '80s seems extraordinary. But so it is with THE SUN'S EYE: so much so that its publishers have requested a revised edition. Given the book's content, its continuing vitality is not extraordinary at all. For, as one of the earliest school collections of work by West Indian writers it was able to draw on some of the very best writing from the region. Stories such as Timothy Callender's *An Honest Thief* and Ralph Prince's *Sharlo's Strange Bargain*, poems such as Edward Kamau Brathwaite's *The Pawpaw* and A. L. Hendriks' *An Old Jamaican Woman Thinks About the Hereafter*, extracts such as those from George Lamming's *In the Castle of My Skin* and from Namba Roy's *Black Albino*, first made available to a young readership through THE SUN'S EYE, are now firm favourites in schools wherever West Indian literature is studied.

THE SUN'S EYE's long history began when I was teaching English to the first three forms of a girls' secondary school in Jamaica. In the early '60s, even with Independence so close, and with a fair quantity of good literature from Jamaica and the other West Indian countries already published, books by British authors alone were read in schools. This seemed to me unnatural, unfair and short-sighted: I wanted my students to be able to read stories and poems about people and places which they recognised, or experiences which were close to them. Also, I was myself an avid reader of West Indian writing, and wanted them to share my pleasure. I therefore read aloud to my students stories, poems, extracts from novels by West Indian writers which I thought they would like. Their response to this writing, their quickened interest in all that they then read, the improvement in what they then wrote — all this encouraged me to make a collection of West Indian writing for young readers in the region.

In this new edition I welcome the chance to make changes recommended to me by teachers, and to include work by younger and more recently-published writers. Here are the features of this new edition:

* again, both stories and poems are included, in the belief that they should be seen as a continuum of writing, and that poetry is not, as is sometimes feared, something strange and obscure. Stories and poems are now placed alternately, and in a new sequence.

* more than half the original contents, including all the firm favourites, have been retained. Other stories and poems, found by students to be less immediately accessible and drawing a less vivid response, have been replaced by six new stories or extracts from novels, and seven new poems: by older writers whose writing was (unbelievably now) not represented here before — Louise Bennett, Mervyn Morris, Earl Lovelace, and by younger writers — Michael Aubertin, Hazel Campbell, Lorna Goodison, Fred D'Aguiar, Clyde Hosein, John Robert Lee, Grace Nichols, Olive Senior.

* the inclusion of Louise Bennett's poem and Olive Senior's story signals the breakthrough in permitted language forms. When I first submitted **THE SUN'S EYE** for publication, in 1962, it was rejected because some of the writing was in 'dialect'. By the time of publication in 1968, dialogue in 'dialect' was permitted, but no work written entirely in what was still considered a debased language form. Now that attitudes to language have been sensibly revised, and that much of the good new Caribbean writing is in 'nation language', more such writing has been included.

* there are still no introductory notes, but there are — in response to persistent demand — three or four questions on each piece of writing: questions which first test surface comprehension, then provoke a search for deeper meaning, then stimulate an oral or written response to the writing.

* as before, the notes on the contributors have been written, or updated, by the authors themselves. The aim is to let the writers speak directly to the students, so that they seem accessible and real, and so that their writing is shown to be part of their lives, rooted in the particular. In response to comments by teachers, authors have attempted to describe the occasion and context of each piece of writing.

*   these 'Notes about the Writers', and the questions, are deliberately not placed beside each story or poem, but at the back of the book. This continues the accepted style of **THE SUN'S EYE**, where the writing itself is uncluttered by notes, in the hope that the students' response may be fresh and direct. The questions follow the order of the contents, with a page reference; the 'Notes about the Writers' are in alphabetical order by author.

Each time I return to the Caribbean — my most recent visits were in 1981 and 1986 — I meet teachers who say their students have enjoyed and benefited from using **THE SUN'S EYE**. This new edition is dedicated to them: for keeping faith with the concept of the book, and for making this new edition possible.

Again, as before, I must thank many people: the writers, especially those who have been in the book from the start, and who have so kindly agreed that their work should continue to be in it; the teachers, who have advised and encouraged me: Veronica Jenkin initially, and more recently Liz Gerschel and Dorothy Noel, who have given me many specific suggestions on the contents, and given practical help with the questions. I thank in particular Edward Kamau Brathwaite for his creative interest when the book was first put together, Mervyn Morris for his valuable help with preparing the new edition; and Arthur Seymour for his long-standing encouragement, and for permission to take my title from his poem, 'For Christopher Columbus':

> In the vast Atlantic
> The sun's eye blazes over the edge of ocean
> And watches the islands in a great bow curving
> From Florida down to the South American coast.

And finally, warm thanks always to my pupils at Westwood High School, Jamaica, and the late Dorothy Parsons, then headmistress, without whom **THE SUN'S EYE** would never have come into being.

Anne Walmsley
London 1987

Poems and Stories

Hymn to the Sea

Frank A. Collymore

Like all who live on small islands
I must always be remembering the sea,
Being always cognizant of her presence; viewing
Her through apertures in the foliage; hearing,
When the wind is from the south, her music, and
   smelling
The warm rankness of her; tasting
And feeling her kisses on bright sunbathed days;
I must always be remembering the sea.

Always, always the encircling sea,
Eternal: lazylapping, crisscrossed with stillness;
Or windruffed, aglitter with gold and the surf;
Waist-high for children, or horses for Titans;
Her lullaby, her singing, her moaning; on sands,
On shingle, on breakwater, and on rock;
By sunlight, starlight, moonlight, darkness:
I must always be remembering the sea.

Go down to the sea upon this random day
By metalled road, by sandway, by rockpath,
And come to her. Upon the polished jetsam,
Shell and stone and weed and saltfruit
Torn from the underwater continents, cast
Your garments and despondencies; re-enter
Her embracing womb: a return, a completion.
I must always be remembering the sea.

Life came from the sea, and once a goddess arose
Fullgrown from the saltdeep; love
Flows from the sea, a flood; and the food
Of islanders is reaped from the sea's harvest.
And not only life and sustenance; visions, too,
Are born of the sea; the patterning of her rhythm
Finds echoes within the musing mind.
I must always be remembering the sea.

Symbol of fruitfulness, symbol of barrenness,
Mother and destroyer, the calm and the storm!
Life and desire and dreams and death
Are born of the sea; this swarming land
Her creation, her signature set upon the salt ooze
To blossom into life; and the red hibiscus
And the red roofs burn more brightly against her blue.
I must always be remembering the sea.

Catching Crabs

George Lamming

Boy Blue left us and crept towards the crabs, approaching them from the back. Crab-catching was a pastime which we used to test our speed as well as lightness of touch. After heavy rains the village was often invaded by crabs, large blue-black creatures sprawling stupidly here and there to get their bearings. The men and boys came out in droves with sticks and pokers and traps of every description. Children and women screamed when they saw the catch. Sometimes it yielded hundreds of crabs, and the boys and men who had trapped them made a prosperous business. Even those who had condemned crab-catching as a dirty sport bought them. They were delicious if you prepared them well. But these crabs that leaned uncertainly on the slope of the shore were different. They were very small and decorous, like cups and saucers which my mother bought and put away. You couldn't use them for drinking purposes. They were too delicate and decorous. These little crabs had that quality. Small, enchanting bits of furniture with which the shore was decorated. You wouldn't eat them although the meat might have been as delicious as that of the big village crabs, which were ugly and gross in their crawling movements.

Boy Blue didn't really want to eat one of these. He wanted to catch them as a kind of triumph. He could show what he had done after spending so many hours on the other side of the lighthouse. Catching things gave us little boys a great thrill. Sometimes we shot birds and carried them exposed in the palm of the hand. Everyone could see what we had done, meaning what we had achieved. It was like talking to the fisherman, or climbing a mountain which no one had hitherto dared ascend. The thrill of capturing something! It was wonderful! Boy Blue looked like a big crab crawling on all fours, and he made us laugh with the shift and shake of his slouching movements.

The crabs dropped their eyes and remained still. It was always very difficult to tell what a crab would do. Sometimes they would scamper wildly if you were a mile away, and at other times they would crouch and bundle themselves together the nearer you approached. They seemed to feel that they were unseen because their eyes were dropped level in the slot that contained them. Boy Blue lay flat on the sand with his hands stretched out full length. The crabs were trying to make a way in the sand. They had seen him but there was no great hurry in escaping. Perhaps the sand was their domain. They could appear and disappear at will while you waited and watched. His hands had them covered but there was no contact. The difficulties had only started.

When you were catching a crab with bare hands you required great skill. You had to place your thumb and index finger somewhere between the body and the claws of the crab. That was very tricky, since the crabs' claws were free like revolving chairs. They could spin, it seemed, in all directions, and they raised and dropped them to make any angle. Hundreds of boys were squeezed time and again in their effort to trap the crabs barehanded. If you missed the grip, or gripped a minute too soon the claws had clinched you. And the claws cut like blades. You had to know your job. You had to be a crab catcher, as we would say.

A master at the art, Boy Blue considered he was. He had caught several in his time. The art had become a practised routine. It was simply a matter of catching them. In this art he carried the same assurance and command we had noticed in the fisherman. He lay flat with his hands pressed on the crabs' back. He was trying to gather them up all together. His thumb had found the accustomed spot between the claw and the body of the crab. The crabs were still but buckled tight, so that it was difficult to strengthen the grip. Sometimes they seemed to understand the game. They remained still and stiffly buckled, and when you least expected the claws flashed like edged weapons.

The waves came up and the sand slid back. It seemed they would escape. If the waves came up again the sand would be loosened and they could force a way easily into the sand. Boy Blue had missed his grip. The wave came again and the sand sloped. Boy Blue slid back and the crabs were free from his grip. He propelled his feet in the sand in an attempt to heave himself forward. His weight pressed down. The wave receded and the sand shifted sharply. He came to a kneeling position and the sand slipped deeper. The crabs were safe. He threw his hand up and stood. The sand shifted under his feet and the waves hastening to the shore lashed him face downward. The salt stung his eyes and he groped to his feet. Another wave heaved and he tottered. The crabs! The crabs had disappeared. We could not understand what was happening. Boy Blue was laughing. It made us frightened the way he laughed. A wave wrenched him and now he was actually in the sea. We shivered, dumb. A wave pushed him up, and another completing the somersault plunged him down. He screamed and we screamed too. He was out of sight and we screamed with all the strength of our lungs. And the waves washed our screams up the shore. It was like a conspiracy of waves against the crab catcher.

We screamed and the fisherman came out from behind the lighthouse. We motioned him to the spot where we had last seen Boy Blue. There was a faint scream in the air. We could not understand how it had happened. We could not follow the speed of the fisherman's movements. He had gathered up the net and tossed it in the sea over the area we had indicated. He hauled earnestly and the body of the net emerged with the strangest of all catches. Boy Blue was there. He was rolled up like a wet blanket. We were dumb with fright. He looked so impotent in the net. His eyes were bloodshot and his body heaved with a great flood of wind. He gasped and gasped, like a dog that had strained itself with too great speed in the chase.

The fisherman hauled him up the beach and emptied the net as if it contained a useless dead thing. He looked at Boy Blue with a kind of disgust. Boy Blue was like a fly which had buzzed too long. You slapped it down and were sorry that you made such a mess of your hands. You might have left it. But you couldn't. It was unbearable. A necessary evil. The fisherman looked down at Boy Blue, unspeaking. There was no trace of what we could call bad temper. Just a kind of quiet disgust. Boy Blue sat silent, his teeth chattering and his whole body a shiver of flesh in the wind. We could not speak. We were afraid of the fisherman. The way he looked at us! He was like someone who had been sorry for what he did, and yet not sorry since he knew it had to be done. He looked so terribly repentant and at the same time there was an expression which we could not define. Under the marble eyes and the impenetrable stare there must have been something that cried out for life. He knew the catch was not a fish, but he hauled the net with the earnestness that could only have meant a desire beyond his control for the other's survival. Now he looked so terribly penitent. We were frightened.

"I should have let you drown," he snarled, and his voice held terror.

"Thank you, sir," Boy Blue said, catching his breath. It was the first time Boy Blue had spoken.

"By Christ, you should have drown," the fisherman snarled again.

"You mustn't say that," Boy Blue said. We were stunned by the impertinence of the words. But there couldn't have been impertinence. Boy Blue was shivering like a kitten that had had a bath.

"Why the hell shouldn't I have let you drown?" the fisherman shouted. It was the first thing he had said that made us think he was really human like us. The way he said it! He now looked angry.

8

"Tell me," he snapped. "Tell me to my face why the hell I shouldn't have let you drown?"

"Cause if I'd drown I couldn't have been able to tell you thanks," Boy Blue said. He was serious and the fisherman walked back towards the lighthouse.

.   .   .   .   .

The little crabs had appeared again. Boy Blue looked at them and as quickly looked away.

"Don't look that way," he said, and led us by the arms towards the other side of the lighthouse.

from **IN THE CASTLE OF MY SKIN**

Bird

Dennis Scott

That day the bird hunted an empty, gleaming sky
and climbed and coiled and spun measures of joy,
half-sleeping in the sly wind way
above my friend and me. Oh,
its wings' wind-flick and fleche were free
and easy in the sun, and a whip's tip
tracing of pleasure its mute madrigal,
that I below watched it so tall
it could not fall save slow
down the slow day.

"What is it?" said my friend.
"Yonder . . ."
                    Hill and home patterned and curved
and frozen in the white round air
"Yes, there," he said, "I see it — "

                                        up

the steep sky till the eye
lidded from weight of sun on earth and wing!

"Watch this," he said, bending for stones,
and my boy's throat grew tight with warning
to the bird that rode the feathered morning.

"Now there's a good shot, boy!" he said.
I was only ten then.
"If you see any more be sure to shout
but don't look at the sun too long," he said,
"makes your eyes run."

An Honest Thief

Timothy Callender

Every village has a "bad man" of its own, and St. Victoria Village was no exception. It had Mr. Spencer. Mr. Spencer was a real "bad man", and not even Big Joe would venture to cross his path. Besides, everybody knew that Mr. Spencer had a gun, and they knew he had used it once or twice too. Mr. Spencer didn't ever go out of his way to interfere with anybody, but everybody knew what happened to anybody who was foolish enough to interfere with Mr. Spencer. Mr. Spencer had a reputation.

Now, at the time I am speaking of, every morning when Mr. Spencer got up, he made the sign of the cross, went and cleaned his teeth, and then left the house and went into the open yard to look at his banana tree. He had a lovely banana tree. Its trunk was beautiful and long and graceful, the leaves wide and shiny, and, in the morning, with the dew-drops glinting silver on them, it seemed like something to worship — at least Mr. Spencer thought so.

Mr. Spencer's wife used to say to him, "Eh, but Selwyn, you like you bewitch or something. Every morning as God send I see you out there looking up in that banana tree. What happen? Is you woman or something? Don't tell me you starting to go dotish."

And Mr. Spencer would say, "Look, woman, mind you own business, eh?" And if she was near him, she would collect a clout around her head too.

So one morning Mrs. Spencer got vexed and said: "You going have to choose between me and that blasted banana tree."

"Okay, you kin pack up and go as soon as you please," Mr. Spencer said.

So Mrs. Spencer went home to her mother. But, all said and done, Mrs. Spencer really loved her husband, so after two days she came back and begged for forgiveness.

Mr. Spencer said: "Good. You have learn your lesson. You know now just where you stand."

"Yes, Selwyn," Mrs. Spencer said.

"That is a good banana tree," Mr. Spencer said. "When them bananas ripe, and you eat them, you will be glad I take such good care of the tree."

"Yes, Selwyn," she said.

The banana tree thrived under Mr. Spencer's care. Its bunch of bananas grew and grew, and became bigger and lovelier every day. Mr. Spencer said: "They kin win first prize at any agricultural exhibition, you know, Ellie."

"Yes, Selwyn," she said.

And now, every morning Mr. Spencer would jump out of bed the moment he woke and run outside to look at his banana tree. He would feel the bunch of bananas and murmur, "Yes, they really coming good. I going give them a few more days." And he would say this every day.

Monday morning he touched them and smiled and said: "They really coming good. I going give them couple days more." Tuesday morning he smiled and said, "A couple days more. They really coming good." Wednesday morning — and so on, and so on, and so on.

The lovelier the bananas grew, the more Mrs. Spencer heard of them, all through the day. Mr Spencer would get up from his breakfast and say: "I wonder if that tree all right! Ellie, you think so? Look, you better go and give it little water with the hose." Or, he would wake up in the middle of the night, and rouse his wife and say, "Hey, but Ellie, I wonder if the night temperature ain't too cold for the tree! Look, you best had warm some water and put it to the roots . . . along with some manure. Go 'long right now!" And Mrs. Spencer would have to obey.

One morning Mr. Spencer came in from the yard and said as usual, "Ellie girl, them bananas real lovely now. I think I going pick them in couple days' time."

"Always 'couple days'," she said, peeved. "Man, why you don't pick them now quick before you lose them or something? You ain't even got no paling round the yard. Suppose somebody come in here one o' these nights and t'ief them?"

"T'ief which?" Mr. Spencer said. "T'ief which? T'ief which?"

The truth was, nobody in the village would have dared to steal

Mr. Spencer's bananas, for, as I have mentioned, he was a "bad man".

Then, one day, another "bad man" came to live in the village. He was the biggest and toughest man anybody had ever seen. He had long hairy arms and a big square head and a wide mouth and his name was Bulldog.

Everybody said, "One o'these days Bulldog and Mr. Spencer going clash. Two bad men can't live in the same village." And they told Mr. Spencer, "Bulldog will beat you!"

"Beat who? Beat who? Beat who?" Mr. Spencer said. He always repeated everything three times when he was indignant.

And Bulldog said: "Who this Spencer is? Show him to me."

So one evening they took Bulldog out by Mr. Spencer's, and he came up where Mr. Spencer was watering his tree and said: "You is this Mr. Spencer?"

"How that get your business?" Mr. Spencer asked.

"Well, this is how. If you is this Spencer man, I kin beat you." Bulldog always came straight to the point.

"Who say so? Who say so? Who say so?"

"I say so."

"And may I ask who the hell you is?" Mr. Spencer asked. "Where you come from?"

"You never hear 'bout me?" Bulldog said, surprised. "Read any newspaper that print since 1950, and you will see that I always getting convicted for wounding with intent. I is a master at wounding with intent. I would wound you with intent as soon as I look at you. You wants to taste my hand?"

Mr. Spencer didn't want to, however. He looked Bulldog up and down and said: "Well, I ain't denying you might stand up to me for a few minutes." He paused for a moment, and then said: "But I bet you ain't got a banana tree like mine."

He had Bulldog there. It was true that Bulldog had a banana tree, and, seen alone, it was a very creditable banana tree. But beside Mr. Spencer's it was a little warped relic of a banana tree.

Bulldog said: "Man, you got me there fir truth."

"That ain't nothing," Mr. Spencer said. "Look up there at them bananas."

Bulldog looked. His eyes and mouth opened wide. He rubbed

13

his eyes. He asked: "Wait — them is real bananas?"

"Um-hum," Mr. Spencer replied modestly. "Of course they still a bit young, so if they seem a little small . . ."

'Small!" Bulldog said. "Man, them is the biggest bananas I ever see in my whole life. Lemme taste one."

"One o'which? One o'which? One o'which?"

Bulldog didn't like this. "Look, if you get too pow'ful with me, I bet you loss the whole dam bunch."

"Me and you going get in the ropes over them same bananas," Mr. Spencer said. "I kin see that. And now, get out o' my yard before I wound you with intent and with this same very chopper I got here."

Bulldog left. But he vowed to taste one of Mr. Spencer's bananas if it was the last thing he ever did.

Mrs. Spencer told her husband: "Don't go and bring yourself in any trouble with that jail-bird. Give he a banana and settle it."

"Not for hell," Mr. Spencer said. "If he want trouble, he come to the right place. Lemme ketch him 'round that banana tree. I waiting for he."

"C'dear, pick the bananas and eat them all quick 'fore he come back and t'ief them."

"No," Mr. Spencer said. "I waiting for he. I waiting. Let him come and touch one — just one, and see what he get."

A few days passed. Bulldog had tried to forget Mr. Spencer's bananas, but he couldn't put them out of his mind. He did everything he could to rid his thoughts of that big beautiful bunch of bananas which had tempted him that day in Mr. Spencer's yard.

And then he began to dream about them. He talked about them in his sleep. He began to lose weight. And every day when he passed by Mr. Spencer's land, he would see Mr. Spencer watering the banana tree, or manuring it, or just looking at it, and the bananas would seem to wink at Bulldog and challenge him to come and touch one of them.

One morning Bulldog woke up and said: "I can't stand it no longer. I got to have one o' Spencer's bananas today by the hook or by the crook. I will go and ax him right now." He got up and went to Mr. Spencer.

Mr Spencer was in the yard feeling the bananas. He was saying to himself: "Boy, these looking real good. I going to pick them tomorrow."

Bulldog stood up at the edge of Mr. Spencer's land: he didn't want to offend him by trespassing. He called out: "Mr. Spencer, please, give me one of your bananas."

Mr. Spencer turned round and saw him. He said: "Look, get out o' my sight before I go and do something ignorant."

And Bulldog said: "This is you last chance. If I don't get a banana now, you losing the whole bunch, you hear?"

"But look at . . . But look at . . . But look at . . ." Mr. Spencer was so mad he could scarcely talk.

Now Bulldog was a conscientious thief. He had certain moral scruples. He liked to give his victims a fifty-fifty chance. He said: "I going t'ief you bananas tonight, Spencer. Don't say I ain't tell you."

"You's a idiot?" Mr. Spencer called back. "Why you don't come? I got a rifle and I will clap a shot in the seat o' you pants, so help me."

"Anyhow, I going t'ief you bananas," Bulldog said. "I can't resist it no more."

"Come as soon as you ready, but anything you get you kin tek."

"That is okay," Bulldog said. "I tekking all o' them."

Mr. Spencer pointed to a sign under the banana tree. It read: TRESPASSERS WILL BE PERSECUTED. "And for you, persecuting mean shooting."

Bulldog said nothing more but went home.

A little later in the day, a little boy brought a message on a piece of note-paper to Mr. Spencer. It read, "I will thief your bananas between 6 o'clock tonite and 2 o'clock tomorra morning." Mr. Spencer went inside and cleaned his gun.

Mrs. Spencer said, "But look how two big men going kill theyself over a bunch o' bananas! Why you don't go and pick them bananas *now* and mek sure he can't get them."

"Woman," Mr. Spencer replied, "this is a matter of principle. I refuse to tek the easy way out. Bulldog is a blasted robber and he must be stopped, and I, Adolphus Selwyn McKenzie Hezekiah

15

Spencer, is the onliest man to do it. Now, you go and boil some black coffee for me. I will have to drink it and keep awake tonight if I is to stand up for law and order."

At six o'clock Mr. Spencer sat down at his backdoor with his rifle propped upon the step and trained on the banana tree. He kept his eyes fixed there for the slightest sign of movement, and didn't even blink. It was a lovely moonlight night. "If he think I mekking sport, let him come, let him come, let him come."

Seven, eight, nine, ten, eleven, twelve o'clock. And no sign of Bulldog. And Mr. Spencer hadn't taken his eyes off the banana tree once. In the moonlight the tree stood there lovely and still, and the bananas glistened. Mr. Spencer said, "They real good now. I going pick them tomorrow without fail."

Mrs. Spencer said: "Look, Selwyn, come lewwe go to bed. The man ain't a fool. He ain't coming."

"Ain't two o'clock yet," Mr. Spencer said.

And all the time Mrs. Spencer kept him supplied with bread and black coffee. He took his food with one hand and disposed of it without ever taking his eyes off the tree. The other hand he kept on the gun, one finger on the trigger. He was determined not to take his eyes off that tree.

One o'clock. No Bulldog.
Half past one. No Bulldog.
Quarter to two. No Bulldog.

Mrs. Spencer said: "The man ain't coming. Lewwe go to bed. Is a quarter to two now."

"We may as well wait till two and done now," Mr. Spencer said.

Ten to two. No Bulldog.

"Hell! This is a waste o' good time," Mr. Spencer said.

Five to two.

At one minute to two, Mr. Spencer looked at his wristwatch to make sure and turned his head and said to his wife, "But look how this dam vagabond make we waste we good time."

Then he looked back at the banana tree. He stared. His mouth opened wide. The banana tree stood there empty, and the only indication that it had once proudly displayed its prize bunch of bananas was the little stream of juice that was dribbling down from the bare, broken stem.

Song of the Banana Man

Evan Jones

Tourist, white man, wiping his face,
Met me in Golden Grove market place.
He looked at my old clothes brown with stain
And soaked right through with the Portland rain.
He cast his eye, turned up his nose,
He says, "You're a beggar man I suppose,"
He says, "Boy, get some occupation,
Be of some value to your nation."

I said, "By God and this big right hand
You must recognise a banana man."

Up in the hills, where the streams are cool,
Where mullet and janga swim in the pool,
I have ten acres of mountain side,
And a dainty foot donkey that I ride,
Four Gros Michel, and four Lacatan,
Some coconut trees, and some hills of yam,
And I pasture on that very same land
Five she goats and a big black ram.

That, by God and this big right hand,
Is the property of the banana man.

I leave my yard early morning time
And set my foot to the mountain climb,
I bend my back to the hot-sun toil
And my cutlass rings on the stony soil,
Clearing and weeding, digging and planting,
Till Massa sun drop back of John Crow mountain,
Then home again in cool evening time,
Perhaps whistling this little rhyme,

(*Sing*) "Praise God and my big right hand
I will live and die a banana man."

Banana day is my special day
I cut my stems and I'm on my way.
Load up the donkey, leave the land,
Head down the hill to banana stand.
When the truck comes round I take a ride
All the way down to the harbour side.
That is the night when you, tourist man,
Would change your place with a banana man.

Yes, by God, and my big right hand,
I will live and die a banana man.

The bay is calm, and the moon is bright
The hills look black though the sky is light,
Down at the dock is an English ship,
Resting after her ocean trip,
While on the pier is a monstrous hustle,
Tally men, carriers, all in a bustle,
With stems on their heads in a long black snake
Some singing the songs that banana men make.

Like (*sing*) ''Praise God and my big right hand
I will live and die a banana man.''

Then the payment comes, and we have some fun,
Me, Zekiel, Breda and Duppy Son.
Down at the bar near United wharf,
We knock back a white rum, bust a laugh,
Fill the empty bag for further toil
With saltfish, breadfruit, coconut oil.
Then head back home to my yard to sleep
A proper sleep that is long and deep.

Yes, by God, and my big right hand,
I will live and die a banana man.

So when you see those old clothes brown with stain
And soaked right through with the Portland rain
Don't cast your eyes nor turn your nose,
Don't judge a man by his patchy clothes,
I'm a strong man, a proud man, and I'm free
Free as these mountains, free as this sea,
I know myself, and I know my ways,
And will say with pride to the end of my days.

(*sing*) ''Praise God and my big right hand
I will live and die a banana man.''

Crow

Clyde Hosein

Crow sat in the tall Savannah grass and sang to himself, more softly than in the church, when, wearing his pin-striped Indian whipcord suit, he let his voice warble from the choir loft until the altar hummed with the Ave Maria, Salve Regina or Veni Creator.

He sang in all seven churches in Esperance; his clear baritone was in constant demand. But he preferred the more flexible program of the Protestant churches, where often the songs to mark the ring and register ceremonies were the same as those on the hit parade. When a Presbyterian or Methodist bride requested a song he would happily croon *I Believe, Be my love* or *Where have all the flowers gone*, not only for the two or three dollars the best man pressed into his palm, but also in the hope that he might be launched on his career; for who knew in which congregation lurked the impressario, radio producer or record manufacturer from Port of Spain.

From where he sat Crow saw his father's house crowded with idlers and customers waiting for haircuts and shaves. In the front gallery his brothers and his father, old Kernahan, worked with scissors and razor. Crow could catch on the warm wind the chatter about crab catches, the sugar factory and recent events in Esperance.

Occasionally one of the idlers would go from his seat on one of the long benches in the front, along the side or through the

house, to the back gallery where more young men were playing cards and draughts and members of Dynamos Sports Club were meeting.

Crow watched the bus slow at the STOP sign nailed to the almond tree and heard the men in the front gallery laugh, as they always did, at some strained face at a bus window.

A longing possessed him to escape Esperance, the heat, the cinema, the cricket, the farting contests, the endless punning.

He rose from the grass, adjusted his athletic wrist brace and began to walk towards the house.

"The old Crow," cried the men in the back gallery.

"You cutting hair today, Indian?" asked Dingo.

With a feeling of resignation Crow went to his bedroom and brought out his box of barbering tools. He set it upon the brick balustrade. "Sit down," he told Dingo. He sent the card players with their bench into the yard. He sharpened the razor on the strop that hung from the kitchen wall. From up front, barely audible between joke and exploding laughter, four pairs of scissors clipped in unison.

Lying on his bed he watched the lights of a passing vehicle travel the ceiling. Again he had worked far into the night, writing jingles for products he thought needed such an impetus. He was experimenting with a blend of calypso melody and American rock rhythm.

He had plunged with all his energy into that activity and felt grateful for the advice of the bus driver from Arouca who had been in the chorus for a washing powder radio commercial and soon was leaving for New York.

Crow had spent many months studying the structure of popular jingles like *Brush your teeth with Colgate, Tide's in; dirt's out*, and *You can trust your car to the man who wears the star*. He was sure he had discovered the laws that governed their success.

His thoughts wandered to his earliest attempts at songwriting. He was nearing sixteen and had hoped to sell song poems to Five Star Music Masters, New York or Los Angeles — he still was not sure which.

But he was then too inexperienced to write of love. And despite the localization of the lyrics — keskidee for sparrow, governor-plum for elm, Esperance for San Francisco — every song he produced sounded like one he knew.

When he blew out the lamp the first bus to Port of Spain was straining along the road in the muddy dawn light.

Across the Savannah the grandstand stood dark. Seed-hunting tanagers broke the silence. He felt pride and pity as he watched his brothers' faces. Late the previous evening they had played ninety minutes of football for Dynamos and sent a visitor squad back home with a 7 to 1 licking.

He emptied the bucket of its red almond leaves, filled it at the standpipe, jumped the drain and went along the side of the house to the roofless bathroom. He took off his T-shirt, picked up the tin cup from the stone floor and poured water on his head.

The dawning sun had begun to filigree the wet Savannah grass when, in his whipcord suit, Crow stepped aboard the second bus and sat at the rear.

Two hours later, after they had rattled through canefields and hamlets, he alighted on South Quay and walked along Frederick Street. Only once before, when he had gone to the Red House for his birth certificate, had he been so far into the core of the city. He came to the same intersection twice, and then he found the building on Gordon Street.

Crow approached the bronze directory on the white wall. HUMPHREY, LEWIS & GRAHAM. He checked the name against the card the Arouca bus driver had given him. At the bottom of the card he read: F. A. Alcazar, Account Executive.

Crow looked up at the sunburnt hills. He felt disoriented but had memorized landmarks along the way; he could retrace his steps to the bus stand. He walked along the wall and peered through the pikes that rose through periwinkle and ixora. In the lower Palladian window a young woman was busy at a typewriter.

He walked back to the gate. PUSH said the sign. His heart beat faster and faster. Except for Father Kennedy at Esperance R. C., he had never spoken to a white person.

At noon, when the street overflowed with blue-uniformed schoolgirls and office workers had got into the parked cars and driven away, Crow still stood near the gate with the lyrics of a

Malta stout jingle in the envelope in his hand.

He walked down the street, coming to a cafe on a corner. Behind the counter an old Chinese man was serving black children sandwiches and peanut punch. Crow went in and bought a hops bread and ham.

Not until 2.30 did he summon up the courage to push open the gate. He was halfway up one of the flanking granite stairways when a khaki-clad man challenged him from a dark cubicle under the building.

"Who you come to see here man?"

Crow mumbled something about a wrong address and escaped to the safety of the sidewalk. The sun had stewed the asphalt. He gazed at the bubbles of tar on the pavement as he sat on the kerb with his jacket off.

He went back to the ixora and saw an Indian in a blue uniform standing at the secretary's desk. When the messenger looked out Crow gestured with an upraised hand, which the man correctly assessed as a sign for help, for he came out and Crow gave him the card.

"Why don't you go in and see Mr. Alcazar?" the man rebuked. "Don't you have an appointment?"

When Crow did not reply the man added, "Alright, wait here. I'll find out if he can see you."

Soon the messenger re-emerged with a fistful of letters. "Go up the stairs," he said.

The secretary had come to the door. Crow held out the card and tiptoed behind her. The messenger and the man in the khaki suit stood side by side below, scowling at him.

He sat in the chair at the side of the desk and when Alcazar swung around from the credenza Crow stared into his blue eyes and could not utter a word. He thrust the sheet of paper at Alcazar.

"From Esperance eh." Alcazar read the top of the sheet where Crow had written his name and address below *Respectfully Submitted*. "My uncle was an overseer on the sugar estate there," Alcazar said.

"Radio commercials. I want to make radio commercials sir," Crow blurted. The argument he had practised eluded him, and

24

the more he tried to coordinate his thoughts the more frantic he became. He held his wrist in his hand, covering up his identification bracelet.

Alcazar studied the Malta stout lyrics. "Do you have anything on the air?" he asked.

"No sir, but I sing at weddings." Crow avoided Alcazar's eyes.

"Ah, you sing too. What songs besides those at weddings?"

"The classics sir," Crow answered. "My favourite is Old Cape Cod."

Alcazar smiled. He was much younger than Crow had imagined, with a boyish voice that softened further when he spoke into the telephone, "Is the Turner Tissue recording still on?" Then, addressing Crow, he went on, "Let me put you in the picture, Mr. Kernahan. We employ professional people: copywriters, calypsonians, all kinds of musicians. It's a pity . . ." He handed Crow the lyrics.

". . . because you've sold me on Malta Stout. This is good clean hard-selling copy, but, unfortunately, our staff handles all the writing. However, we are always looking for good singers. Are you interested in a tissue ad?"

"O yes," Crow, at the edge of his seat, replied.

"It'll be an audition, you understand." Alcazar wrote in his desk diary.

"I'll be pleased sir," Crow said.

The first bus took him to the city with hours to spare. He walked the almost deserted streets, found Tragarete Road and headed north.

Above a grocery he saw the sign, CALDERON STUDIOS. He sat under an old samaan tree in the square opposite and watched the street come to life.

The technician arrived and let in the men who had been waiting at the door. Crow crossed the street and followed them up the stairs. He sat, as directed, in the studio and studied the typewritten lyrics.

The band began to play and Alcazar arrived. The band-leader hummed a few bars for the benefit of the singers.

The technician said, "Singer one, take one," and the band-leader called the first man to the microphone.

Crow listened to performer after performer. He found it difficult to swallow. And then his turn came.

He sang erratically, forcing the musicians to change pace to keep in time. Alcazar, sitting with the technician behind the glass panel in the control room, added to his unease.

"I'll phone you," Alcazar said through the partly-opened door. The eighth singer was getting ready.

"I don't have a phone."

"I'll write you then."

Down the stairs, on the long walk to the stand, and sitting in the bus watching the ajoupas and cane patches fly by, Crow's dislocated brain replayed the lines he had fluffed:

> We have the tissue for every issue
> Cold, fever, cough and ague
> Turner's Tissue for you.

The rainy season came. The drain below the front gallery gurgled all day. Sometimes a truck or a taxi sped through the puddles and a fine mist blew into the gallery where Crow and his father and brothers worked, surrounded by chatter and horseplay. Crow wanted to run into the rain, far from the overrun house.

He said, "I cut my last head for the day." He took his toolbox in. He emptied his pockets on his bed and counted the money. Three dollars; twelve customers.

He walked across the Savannah through the midget football game, listening to the squelch of his shoes.

The sun came out suddenly, and before he reached the grandstand the water on the asphalt walkways began to evaporate in curling wisps. He sat in the top tier and watched the boys kick the football to the canefield. He went from thought to thought and dark came down.

It gave him a thrill to sit in one place and watch the earth change. Across the fields, in the canecutters' mud hutments orange flambeaux flared. Stars began to show in the powder-blue sky. A bullfinch flew down to the lowest tier.

A great sadness overcame him; yet, he began to sing: *And the little señorita*.

He sang for the croaking frogs, for the cane, the Savannah, the poor people huddled before their rag-and-bottle lamps, for his dead mother, the boredom and materialism of Esperance: *You're breaking my heart; Unforgettable; Some enchanted evening.*

When the moon rose over the guava trees he thought of other lands where the same light spread its ghostly sheet, of breakers foaming on white beaches and people going home from work. He thought of different ways of life, of women, of love. He cried as he sang *Green eyes, Lady of Spain, No other love.*

The last bus had gone and the road was deserted. He got up and stood for a long time before he walked across the moonlit grass towards the shadowed house.

In the morning the letter came. As soon as the postman put it in his hand Crow ran far into the Savannah, tearing at the envelope. In it was a cheque for $15; and the letter:

> Dear Mr. Kernahan,
> Thank you for your audition tape for our client's product, Turner's Tissue.
> We enclose the standard fee of fifteen dollars.
>
> Best wishes, F. A. Alcazar

Sunday. The gathering had begun. The young men, bleary-eyed from graveyard shifts at the sugar factory, crammed the galleries. Some sat with their buttocks overhanging the balustrade. If one lost his balance he would plunge to the concrete drain with its ribbon of water.

Old Kernahan leaned across the drain near the almond tree. He had his scissors and comb in hand and talked to the policeman who sat on his bicycle with one foot resting on the kerb. Kernahan cackled with glee when the corporal told him how difficult it was for couples to find a singer for their weddings.

Dingo drove up in his fish van. He rolled down the window and shouted, "Mr. K., what's the latest from the old Crow?"

"I was telling the corporal," Kernahan said, "Crow's doing really well. He got another promotion. Assistant Night Shift Supervisor. Get that, *Supervisor!* The man's top brass in that factory in Leeds."

Case-History, Jamaica

Mervyn Morris

In 19-something X was born
in Jubilee Hospital, howling, black.

In 19- (any date plus four)
X went out to school.
They showed him pretty pictures
of his Queen.

When he was 7, in elementary school,
he asked what naygas were.
In secondary school he knew.
He asked in History one day
where slaves came from.
"Oh, Africa," the master said,
"Get on with your work."

Up at the university he didn't find himself;
and, months before he finally dropped out,
would ramble round the campus late at night
and daub his blackness on the walls.

Ascot

Olive Senior

"That Ascot goin go far," Mama say, "Mark my word."

"Yes. Him goin so far him goin ennup clear a prison," Papa say. Every time you mention Ascot name to Papa these days the big vein in Papa forehead tighten up and you know he trying hard to control himself.

"Oh gawd when all is said an done the bwoy do well Jackie. Doan go on so," Mama say.

"De bwoy is a livin criminal. Do well me foot. Look how him treat him family like they have leprosy. Deny dem. Is so you wan you pickney behave. Cho woman. Yu was always a fool," and with that Papa jam him hat on him head and take off down the road.

See here! I dont think Papa ever recover from the day that Ascot come back. This Ascot is a tall red bwoy that born round here. Mama and all the rest of the women did like Ascot who is Miss Clemmy outside son for Ascot come out with fair skin and straight nose and though him hair not so good it not so bad neither. And nobody know who Ascot father is but is not Dagoman who Miss Clemmy living with all these years for you only have to look at Dagoman to see that.

Anyhow this Ascot tall no langilalla and him not so bad looking though him have a mouth so big that when him smile him lip curl but all the women melt when Ascot smile and say how him bound to go far.

But all that the men remember bout Ascot is that Ascot is a real ginnal and also that Ascot have the biggest foot that anybody round here ever see. Especially Papa.

One time Papa use to miss all kind of thing from the buttery. Now when Papa not looking all we children would tief in there and take two finger ripe banana or some small thing but nothing serious. Papa would find out and accuse we and we would lie but none of we could lie so good because Mama use to beat the lying out of we and Papa would know the culprit right away so nobody would take it serious. Papa use to say he wouldn't grudge his own children nothing, but is the principle of the thing and he dont like to have his authority undermine and that sort of thing.

Well, anyway, one time a whole heap of big thing start disappear from the buttery — a brand new cutlass, some yam head, a crocus bag and finally, a big bunch of banana that Papa was ripening for the church Harvest Festival. Well sah, all we children used to run in the buttery and look at the bunch of banana till we eye water but none of us would bold enough to touch it for is the most beautiful thing that we ever see in our whole life.

So the Saturday morning before the Harvest Festival one bangarang no bus at the house! Papa go into the buttery and the whole bunch of banana no gone way clean. Jesus. You should hear the noise he make. Then him calm down and he just stand there a look at the ground for a long time and is sad we think Papa sad for is the best bunch of banana that he ever grow. But finally him say, "All right. Is Ascot do it. See him guilt there plain as day. Is Ascot one have foot that size." And is true for we all look at the footprint on the ground and we know is Ascot do it.

Papa say to we, "Doan say a word," and him send off to call Ascot while him close the buttery door and tell all of we go sit on the verandah like nothing happen. So Ascot come grinning as usual like him expecting food and Papa say, "Come Ascot me bwoy Harvest Festival pospone and we gwine nyam banana cann done tidday."

As Papa say the word "banana" Ascot not grinning so wide again and he say as if him deaf "Wha Mass Jackie?" and we all start giggle for him voice come out squeaky like muss-muss and Papa say, "Yes bwoy feas tidday." Then we all walk round to the buttery and Papa throw the door wide open and the first thing that everybody see is the hook where the banana was hanging up empty as night.

"Oh gawd where me Harvest Festival banana gaan-o," Papa shout out. "Ascot look ya me banana no gaan."

"Wha Mass Jackie," Ascot say but you could see that him hanging back. "Nutten could go so afta nobody bolnuf come in ya and walk weh wid yu banana."

Papa just stand there for a while as if him studying the situation and then him say, "Ascot me bwoy, yu and me gwine have to play poleece an search fe clues."

Meanwhile Papa there looking at the ground and then he make as if him just see the footprint and he say, "Ascot look here me bwoy," and by now Ascot look like shame-me-lady macca that just done step on. Papa say, "But wait Ascot. Puddon yu foot ya."

And Ascot bawl out "Laaad Mass Jackie is nuh me do it sah."

Papa say, "No? Den puddon yu foot ya yu tiefing brute," and make to grab after Ascot. But Ascot jump back so braps and fly off like streak lightning. And from that day on, Papa swear that him wash him hand of Ascot.

Ascot stay far from the house for a good while and anytime he see Papa him take off to bush for Papa walking bout and threatening to shoot him for him banana though you know after a time that Papa enjoying himself so much telling everybody how him frighten Ascot that you can see that him dont mind bout the banana so much after all. But Ascot really have no shame at all and little by little him start hang round the kitchen again when Papa not there and Mama would feed him till finally him round the house almost as often as before.

Anyway my big brother Kenny did come up from May Pen one Sunday and Ascot come up to him when Papa back turn and ask if he couldnt give him job as gardener. And as Kenny dont know bout the banana — and he must be the only person Papa forget to tell — Kenny say alright. And although Papa warn Kenny that him talking up trouble Mama say that at heart Ascot is really a decent honest boy and that all he need is opportunity so when Kenny ready to leave Ascot arrive with him bundle and seat himself off in Kenny car please no puss!

"No matter how hard yu wuk an how much money yu make yu will nevva find shoes for dem doan mek dem in fe yu size," was Papa's last word to Ascot.

Well sah, as Papa predict Ascot dont stay long with Kenny. Little after Ascot gone there we get letter from Kenny say he sending Ascot home for Ascot dont want do nothing round the yard and all he do all day is jump behind the wheel of motor car the minute people back turn and make noise like say he driving. The letter arrive one day and the next day we get another letter say Ascot take his belonging and a few other things that didnt belong to him so maybe he on the way home and good riddance. Anyway, Ascot never turn up at all and Miss Clemmie getting ready to go out of her mind that he in trouble till she get message say Ascot in Kingston learning to drive.

Then one day, bout a year after, who arrive but Ascot. He wearing a shirt and tie and pants that too short but is alright because it allow you to see Ascot shoes better. Ascot no get shoes! See here, he wearing the biggest pair of puss boot that ever make. It big so till everybody from miles around run to look at Ascot foot in shoes like is the eight wonder of the world. Ascot tell we he driving car in Kingston though most people dont believe him. But mark you, from Ascot small he used to tell me how him life ambition was to dress up in white clothes and drive a big white car.

So Ascot stay round for a while doing not a thing and he not smiley-smiley so much and in fact Ascot get very quiet. Then one day him no announce that him get paper to go States as farm worker and the next day him leave us again dress up in him big brown puss boots.

Well it look like Ascot dead fe true this time for nobody hear from him till government send a man down to Miss Clemmie to find out if she hear from him for he skip the farm work in Florida and just disappear right after he reach. Poor Miss Clemmie frighten so till and crying the whole time now for Ascot for the man say that they going to prison Ascot if they find him for he does do a criminal thing. But still not a word from Ascot and everybody give him up for dead or prison except Papa who say that the cat which is the incarnation of the devil have nine life and that is Ascot. About three year pass and Miss Clemmie no get letter from the United States. She beg me read it to her and it say:

Dear Ma wel i am her in New York is Big plase and they have plenty car I am going to get one yr loving son Ascot.

And he enclose one dollar and no return address. About two year pass and then Miss Clemmie get another letter from the USA which she beg me read. Is from Ascot and it say:

Dear mother wel here I am in Connecticut. Connecticut is Big plais. I driveing car two year now but is not wite yr loving son Ascot.

And he sent two dollar. Then about a year later she get another letter that say:

Dear Mother Chicago is Big plais I drevein wite car for a wite man but he don make me where wite is black unform so I mite leave yr loving son Ascot.

And he send three dollar. "He-he," say Papa to Miss Clemmie, "by the time yu get fifty letter yu nuh rich." But Miss Clemmie dont laugh for she say she sure Ascot leading bad life. And that was the last time she get letter from Ascot.

After that so much time pass that all of we almost forget Ascot. One time Papa did get a little banana bonus so I go to town and come back with some nice meat and Papa go dig him good yam and the day after that we cook a backra dinner. Papa just sitting on the verandah making the smell kill him and telling me and Mama to hurry up. Next thing we know a big white car no draw up at the gate and turn into the yard. "Eheh is who dat?" Papa say and we all run to the verandah. All we can see is the front door open and two foot stick outside.

"Jesus have mercy is Ascot," Mama say, "is Ascot one have foot big so."

"Ascot me teet. Whe Ascot fe get big car from?" Papa say.

But lo and behold. No Ascot! Ascot dress in white from head to toe and though him plenty fatter him teeth kin same way. And a woman get out of the car with him and you can see she foreign from the clothes she wearing and the colour of her hair though I swear afterward is wig.

Eh-eh, Ascot him no rush up to my mother and start hug and kiss her, "Aunt Essie, Aunt Essie," he crying.

"Aunt Essie," Papa say, "since when she anything but Miss Essie," but Ascot rushing to him a cry "Uncle Jackie" and next thing we know he hugging Papa who turn purple he so vex. "Cousin Lily" — thats me he talking to — and he there hugging me too before I know what is happening. Papa stand there with him mouth open like him seeing rolling calf but Ascot so busy a chat he dont notice.

"An this," he say, "is my wife Anthea" and the lady say hello in this deep American accent.

"Ascot then is really you," Mama saying and she look like she almost crying.

"Yes Aunt Essie is real wonderful to see you," Ascot say and his American accent so thick you could cut it with knife.

"Cousin Lily" he say, taking my hand, "Can I speak to you for a minute?" and he haul me off into the parlour. "Cousin Lily, you are my friend for a long time now. Right?" So I say "right." "Okay, so just pretend that you is my cousin and this is my house, right." Eheh I dont know what Ascot playing but this whole thing sweet me so I say OK and call Mama and tell her. Of course she dont understand what really going on so I keep my finger cross.

By the time I get back to the verandah Ascot is there like a man that make out of nothing but energy, is not the Ascot that leave here at all. He just walking and talking and moving his hand up and down the whole time. Then he say to the wife, "Come let me show you around my birthhouse," and next thing he leading her through the whole house as if is him own it. Mama just stand there with her jaw drop and Papa mouth set while the vein in him forehead beating hard. Then Ascot take the wife into the yard and he there waving him hand and telling her. "And this is my property and this is my coconut tree — you ever see coconut tree with coconut before — and this is where I does bathe when I small and this is our water tank that I did help build."

See ya pappyshow! Well that was bad enough but next thing he gone to Papa cocoa tree and he there saying "And this is a cocoa tree from which you does get chocolate bet you never see that before," and he grab up Papa cutlass and chop off one of the cocoa pod and start cut it up to show her the seed.

Papa start to get up but Mama say "Jackie" and he just sink back down into the chair as if he defeated. Then Ascot and him wife came back on the verandah and sit down and Ascot cock up him foot on the railing. He start chatting away but Papa not opening him mouth and so Mama and me there carrying on conversation. Ascot say him driving him own big white car and he work in a garage but he like one of boss man now and he so happy that he had to bring his wife back to show her the birthplace where he spend his happy childhood. He also say they staying in hotel in Kingston and they going back that night and is rent they rent the car they driving. That was one thing but next thing I go ask the wife what she do and she announce that she is really a teacher but right now she just finishing up her Master Degree. Master Degree? — Ascot marry woman with Master Degree and he dont even finish third standard in school. See here Lord. We all speechless again.

So Ascot there chatting and chatting and we all getting hungrier and hungrier and the food smelling better and better and it dont look as if they out to leave so finally Mama say in her best speaky-spokey voice, "Would you like a bite to eat?" and I know is show off she showing off on Ascot wife who have Master Degree that she have good food in the house.

"Yes thank you Aunt Essie is long time since I taste you cooking," Ascot say and cross him leg. Papa give Mama such a look that thank God none of them did see. Mama never see neither she so please that she entertaining somebody with Master Degree for the highest qualified person she ever meet is Extension Officer and that dont count because is only agriculture him did learn. So we put out all the food that we did cook and Mama take out her best crockery and send down to Miss Melda to borrow the glasses that she did just get from her daughter-in-law in the States and everybody sit down to eat — everybody except Papa who say he not hungry and he dont want anything to eat and we know better than to argue with him when he vex like that.

Well sah. Ascot put down a piece of eating there that I couldn't describe to you and when he done the table clean as a whistle. As soon as they eat done Mama say, "Well Ascot I suppose you want to spend some time with Clemmie," and Ascot say "Clemmie — Oh yes" as if he just remember her and he jump up and say "soon be back" and drive off to see Miss Clemmie. I tell you that was the biggest piece of extraness I ever see because Miss Clemmie live in the next bend in the road and if we want to call her all we do is lean out the kitchen window and shout. But Ascot drive gone and he stay away a long time and I believe is to confuse him wife that Miss Clemmie live a long way away.

About half an hour afterward Ascot arrive with the car full with Miss Clemmie and Dagoman and all the children dress in their best clothes. Ascot say to him wife, "And this is Clemmie and Dagoman," and Dagoman lift his hat and bow and I swear Miss Clemmie drop a curtsey.

"Oh and do you live nearby?" say the wife to Miss Clemmie.

"Yes maam, jus round de corner."

"And are all these your children?"

"Yes'm Hascot is de heldes but is not de same fader."

The wife give Ascot a look to kill and is plain she never realise that is Ascot mother.

"But I did almost grow with Aunt Essie" Ascot say quick but you could see him turning red.

"Clemmie," my mother call her inside, "Look here Clemmie," she tell her, "is your daughter-in-law that what you calling her maam for. Dont keep on saying yes maam no maam to everything she say. You hear me."

"Yes maam," say Miss Clemmie and while I inside clearing the table all I can hear is Miss Clemmie saying "yes maam, no maam" to everything her daughter-in-law saying.

Miss Clemmie keep on looking at Ascot as if he is stranger and Dagoman sit on the bench outside as if he too fraid to come near the lady. The children start play round the car and make as if to open the door and Ascot snap at them so till my mother had to say "Hi Ascot is your own little brothers yu treating so."

"Half brother," Ascot say.

From then on things just get from bad to worse. Ascot look like he vex cant done at Clemmie and the wife and stepfather look like they vex cant done with Ascot. So finally Ascot say, "Come let me take you all home for I have to get back to Kingston tonight." But by this time Dagoman face set and he say he prefer to walk and Miss Clemmie and the children get into the car alone and even though Miss Clemmie look like she going to cry you can still see that she feeling proud to have her son driving her in car. But as they drive off all we can hear is Ascot a shout at the children to take their dirty feet off the car seat.

By the time Ascot get back he grinning all over again but you can see that everybody feeling kind of shame and just waiting for him to go. So he finally jump up and start kiss we goodbye only when he put out his hand to Papa Papa wouldnt take it though he shake hands with the wife and talk nice to her for he say afterward that she was a nice mannersable woman and is a shame that she mix up with a criminal like Ascot. So at long last Ascot and his wife drive off the way they did come with plenty horn blowing and hand waving.

Mama was the only one that wave back though and long after the car out of sight she there waving and smiling. "That Ascot," she say, "fancy that. A wife with Master Degree. I did know he was goin get far you know."

"Well he can stay far de next time," Papa shout and walk out of the house.

Next day it all over the district how Miss Clemmie have daughter-in-law with Master Degree and how Ascot prosper and hire big car and staying at hotel in Kingston. But is only me one Miss Clemmie did tell how there was not a bite to eat in the house that day and Ascot never even leave her a farthing. This vex me cant done especially how he did gormandise up all Papa food. So right then and there I start tell her what kind of good-fe-nutten Ascot is. And is only afterward that I realise that Miss Clemmie not listening to a word I saying.

"Dat Hascot. I did always know he wudda reach far yu know," she say almost to herself and her eyes shining like ackee seed.

Song for my Son

Lorna Goodison

My son cries
the cats answer
I hover over his sleeping
suspended on his milk-stained breath
I live in fear of his hurt, his death.
The fear is real
if I close my eyes when it is at its height
I see him curled man-in-miniature asleep.
I hover over his milk-stained breath
and listen for its rise
every one an assurance that he is alive
and if God bargains
I strike a deal with him,
for his life I owe you something, anything
but please let no harm come to him.
The cat cries
my son answers
his sleep is short
his stomach hurts.

An Heir for the Maroon Chief

Namba Roy

Tomaso was sitting with his company of warriors on the same spot he had been some months before when Lago picked the row and fought with him. But today Lago was not there.

He looked up and saw a woman coming down the narrow path towards them.

"It is Nahne," cried one of the men, and Tomaso jumped to his feet as he too recognised the visitor to be Nahne, the village midwife. Her visit could have only one meaning — Kisanka!

He could not wait for the old woman to finish the few chains distance between them. As he walked forward with his companions trailing he called out eagerly, "Greetings, Nahne, is it news of Kisanka?"

The midwife suddenly seemed to be more eager to turn tail than to meet the leader and his companions. She was a short stumpy woman with a face full of wrinkles. Her clothing consisted of a long piece of cloth tied at the waist for a skirt, and another around her like a shawl, which she kept in place with a knot. Tomaso waited politely for the woman to speak remembering also that she was old and had come a long way. But now they were face to face, and only a couple of yards between them, yet apart from nodding her head in confirmation of his question, she stood looking like a frightened animal. There was fear in her eyes and as Tomaso saw it his heart went almost up to his mouth. He could no longer restrain himself.

"Kisanka, O Nahne, is she well?" he asked, trying to keep fear

from his voice.

"She is well, Tomaso, and sends greetings." The voice was subdued and the midwife refused to meet the searching eyes of her chief.

"The child, mother . . . has it come?" He could not keep a tremor out of his voice and his fists opened and closed as he waited for a reply.

"The child has come, Tomaso."

It was too much for the brave warrior chief and even his companions seemed to have to hold back their anger at the old woman's reluctance to speak because of the respect they held for the aged.

"Nahne, I do not wish to offend thee whom I respect but I am waiting for the news of my wife and my child."

Apprehension showed over the speaker's whole body. The woman's hand holding the shawl in place was trembling. Tomaso saw it and his spirit sank and yet his thought was for the messenger. He stepped forward and put his strong young arm around her shoulder.

"Nay, do not fear, O Nahne. Thy news has bad things. I see it in the trembling of the hand which holds the cloth. I am ready. Speak, O mother-of-countless-children. I shall not be angry. How could I? It is no fault of thine." He spoke to comfort the woman though his spirit was heavy with sorrow. He felt that the child must have died at birth and that was why the old midwife was afraid to speak. What else could it be? Had she not told him Kisanka was alive and sent greetings? The woman wiped her eyes with a corner of her shoulder covering, and it seemed she took courage at Tomaso's words of comfort for she at last looked up in his face. She had no eyes for the dozen or so men around her, who fidgeted as if they wished they were not present to see their beloved leader's downcast look and the face of the frightened old woman.

"Tell me, Nahne . . . was it . . . was it a man-child?" Tomaso's voice sounded hoarse as he asked and his eyes were above the heads of all towards the peak of the mountain where the village lay.

"It *is* a manchild, Tomaso."

The man stretched his hand and took hold of the old woman's shoulder he had released a while before. This time his hold was so fierce that she winced from the pain but he noticed nothing.

"You said he *is* a manchild, Nahne! Then he yet lives?" he cried eagerly, catching at the ray of hope the single word gave. He bent his knees so as to see better in her face and as she nodded her head in confirmation he lost control of himself.

"Do you hear, O my brothers? I am a father!"

"We hear, Tomaso! We hear!" shouted the men as if their chief was deaf, waving their hands about and almost jumping for joy, for they loved their young leader.

"No more will Lago be able to mock me!" added Tomaso almost to himself.

"The mountain will shake with the gladness of the people, Tomaso!"

"Aye! The drums will talk good talk, Tomaso, this night!"

"He will be mighty like thyself, O my chief!"

"My head grows big at the tidings, O my leader — "

Each warrior had something nice to say, moving forward to press the shoulder of their chief as a sign of congratulation. And yet, as soon as Tomaso had uttered his first words of gladness a chilly feeling came over him, for the old woman, standing humbly to one side, had no look of joy on her face. She had been like a messenger of bad tidings ever since she came and yet he could not see why. She had said Kisanka had sent greetings. This meant that his wife was well after the confinement. The child was alive. It would not have been if it was deformed: being the son of a chief would not have prevented the midwife from doing her traditional duty which even a chief dared not question. On the contrary, being a chief's child would have been all the more reason for a midwife to see that only the physically perfect survived. And yet the old woman stood as if some great evil had shown its head beside the bed of confinement. The men too, after their congratulations, felt that something was wrong and a sudden chilling silence descended on them all.

"Nahne?" The way Tomaso called her brought back the fear on the midwife's face. He saw it and hastened to assure her.

"Do not fear, O mother-of-countless-children. I would not harm thee even if the fault of the evil news was thine."

Again the water came to the old one's eyes. "Thy son is not like thyself, Tomaso, nor like his mother," she blurted out between sobs.

The startled and puzzled chief shook his head: "I do not understand this riddle, Nahne, speak clearer, I ask thee."

The old woman looked up in the face of her chief with pleading watery eyes: "It is his colour, Tomaso, it is not like that of our people."

"Do you mean that it is the colour of the bakra, mother?" asked Tomaso, almost unable to control his feelings. Then brightening up he added: "But no picni has ever been born with the colour of his people, Nahne!"

The old woman looked at her chief with reproof through her tears. "I have brought countless picnies into the world with these hands, Tomaso. I have seen those whose fathers had been bakra and whose mothers were of our people, but this child's face is whiter than that of a bakra; and its hair is like the cotton that comes from the great cotton trees on these hills."

They all saw the agony which came on their leader's face, and embarrassed, they turned their eyes on their bare toes. The old woman, now that she had broken the news, seemed to feel that promise or no promise, she would be punished. She cowered before the dreadful look she saw on the face of her chief, waiting, it seemed, for sentence to be passed on her, and when, after a long interval of silence, he spoke in a gentle voice, even his companions who knew that his rule was devoid of tyranny or terror, marvelled at his ways.

"Come, Nahne, you and I shall climb the hill and see this child who has courage enough to have a colour of his own." He was the only one amongst them who had the courage to smile at his sad joke.

"Come, Nahne," he urged, taking the old woman by an arm. "We must not keep this little warrior waiting."

from BLACK ALBINO

An Old Jamaican Woman thinks about the Hereafter

A. L. Hendriks

What would I do forever in a big place, who
have lived all my life in a small island?
The same parish holds the cottage I was born in, all
my family, and the cool churchyard.

               I have looked
up at stars from my front verandah and have been
   afraid
of their pathless distances. I have never flown
in the loud aircraft nor have I seen palaces,
so I would prefer not to be taken up high nor
rewarded with a large mansion.

            I would like
to remain half-drowsing through an evening light
watching bamboo trees sway and ruffle for a valley-
     wind,
to remember old times but not to live them again;
occasionally to have a good meal with no milk
nor honey for I don't like them, and now and then to
     walk
by the grey sea-beach with two old dogs and watch
men bring up their boats from the water.

               For all this,
for my hope of heaven, I am willing to forgive my
     debtors
and to love my neighbour . . .

                    although the wretch throws
                         stones
at my white rooster and makes too much noise in her
     damn
          backyard.

The Village Washer

Samuel Selvon

Shortly after the last war the laundry situation took a turn for the worse in the village of Sans Souci, a sugar-cane hamlet thirty-odd miles from the capital of Port of Spain in Trinidad. Here Ma Lambee ruled supreme as the only washer in the district, and in her sole supremacy she grew careless after she had established herself.

Ma Lambee was old and black and possessed remarkable strength which seemed to bow her legs so she walked like a duck.

With the declaration of war, she began to be neglectful of collars and sleeves and the folds at the bottom of trousers, which places the villagers always looked to judge her workmanship. If a button broke or came off as she scrubbed the clothing with a corn husk, she no longer bothered to mend it, and if a thin shirt ripped as she kneaded her gnarled hands into the cloth, she swore the tear was there before she got the shirt. Was a time when she used four bars of blue soap, and if the dirt and perspiration were still stubborn, bought a bit of washing soda and did her best to get the clothes looking clean again. And was a time when she used four to six buckets for two tubs.

Ma Lambee had four flatirons which she heated in a coal pot, wrapping a piece of cloth around the handle to protect her hand as she pressed the clothes. And a good job she did, too, until the war started. Then she bought half the amount of coals and stopped greasing the irons with lard when they were not in use. When she was ironing, she just slid the hot iron around quickly, folded the clothes and put them in the flat, wooden tray, and took them around on her head every Saturday to deliver the laundry.

However, Ma Lambee's excuse that there was a war on didn't stop the villagers from complaining. There were about forty of them living near the canefields where they worked cutting the canes to be transported to the sugar mills two miles away. Of these, about ten did their own washing and the rest depended on

Ma Lambee.

But the old woman paid no attention to the complaints. She always promised to do better the following week, but when she came around balancing the tray on her head, customers discovered all the dirt under the collars, and once a merino was so torn that the owner's wife asked her if it was a net to catch fish in the river, and refused to pay for it.

Ma Lambee was unperturbed. In fact, she was "brazen enough", as a villager put it, to announce that she was raising laundry prices.

"As you know," she told the women as she stopped at each hut to collect the dirty linen, "we fighting a war, and the prices of all things going up. So from now on, I will have to charge more to do up the clothes. Long time a shirt was twelve cents. Now it have to be eighteen cents. And long time, skirt was eighteen cents. Now it have to be a shilling."

From hut to hut, as Ma Lambee passed, words flew furiously.

"Neighbour, you hear about Ma Lambee, how she charging more to do up the clothes now? You can imagine that? And look how careless she getting, not even bothering to sew up a tear, or put back on a button!"

"Yes, is true! I only wish we had another washer in the village; she is the only one, that is why she getting on so!"

"Well, I for one going and try to do the washing myself, if I have time in the evening. The woman must be mad or something!"

"She say the war cause it — what war she talking about?"

A delegation of housewives visited Ma Lambee where she lived in a broken-down hut under a mango tree, and there was a great argument which lasted for two hours. At the end of that time, the women retreated making threats and shaking their fists at Ma Lambee, who had told them flatly that they could do their own nasty washing if they didn't like her terms.

She lost five customers the following week, but the others were forced to put up with her conditions. Ma Lambee smiled to herself as she went about her washing.

But while she was having her own way word of the villagers' plight reached another hamlet called Donkey City, and another aged negro woman named Ma Procop migrated to Sans Souci with the hope of taking over the business from Ma Lambee.

The day Ma Procop arrived, she was greeted with shouts and smiles, though the people were cautious not to commit themselves too much, fearing she might turn out to be a second Ma Lambee.

But Ma Procop was a clever woman. The first day she put up a notice in the village shop, saying that she was willing to take in laundry at pre-war prices. She said she was an experienced washer from Donkey City and was out to give complete satisfaction to one and all.

It was a long notice, and the spelling was bad and it wasn't worded exactly that way, but the three people in the village who could read saw it and soon everybody knew.

When Ma Lambee heard about it she waddled over to the shop and stuck up a big piece of cardboard on which she had had the village painter write a few words in red paint, stating that she was negotiating with a firm in the city for a new type of washing-machine which would make old clothes look like new.

There was no electricity in the village, and it was a lie anyway, but for the first time in her life Ma Lambee was afraid of losing her trade.

That Saturday as she made her rounds she did not get even a vest to wash. Within a week she had lost all her customers. She was jeered at and the new washing-machine became a big joke. Even the children made fun of her, shouting out "Wash-up washer!" when they saw her.

If Ma Lambee saw Ma Procop walking down the road, she waddled over to the other side and turned her head as if she were smelling something bad. She looked upon the intruder as a hated enemy and thought up means of recovering her trade and at the same time putting Ma Procop to such shame that she would have to go back to Donkey City in a hurry.

At first she tried spreading lies.

"You know," she told the woman she met by the shop, "that new washer is a nasty woman. She don't even rinse the clothes, and she look so sickly; take care she don't spread disease in the village!"

But Ma Procop's actions soon had the whole village on her side. She even spent a little out of the money she had saved in Donkey City, and worked late in the night sewing on buttons and mending torn clothing. And she made it her business to be friendly, and was especially kind to the children, buying sweets for them and telling them stories.

Ma Lambee now started a malicious rumour that Ma Procop was an obeah woman who changed herself into a blood-sucking animal in the night.

The simple-minded villagers, quick to superstition and belief in omens and evil spirits, became uneasy as the rumour took root.

One night a wounded animal ran into a backyard and left a trail of blood. Next morning Ma Lambee told them:

"Mm, it look like Ma Procop was working overtime last night. I don't know how you people could let that obeah woman live here."

They began to imagine things. Night noises were attributed to an evil spirit, and though no one pointed directly to Ma Procop, there was an uneasy air whenever she was around. Quick to see her advantage, Ma Lambee pressed home the fact that the new washer was unusually fond of children — and that little ones were the favourites of obeah women.

She did more than talk. One night she poured a gallon of poison on to the roots of a big silkcotton tree in the centre of the village, and next day divined that as a result of Ma Procop's evil deeds the tree would die before a week passed.

She began to make a study of black magic in order to set the village against Ma Procop. She collected an odd miscellany of liquids and bones and other paraphernalia, and cleared her hut of mirrors and all objects in the sign of the cross.

Things came to a head when the silkcotton tree died. It just withered up, as Ma Lambee had predicted, and within two weeks it was nothing but a standing skeleton.

The village women got together to discuss the situation.

"It happen just as Ma Lambee say, it look like Ma Procop is really a obeah woman."

"We have to put she to the test — get she to look in a mirror, and make the sign of the cross over she head. If she is really a obeah woman, she can't stand that at all."

Ma Procop in the meantime was well aware of what was going on in the village. Yet she did nothing, except that one morning she went to Donkey City and came back with a parcel under her arm and a small smile on her lips.

Two days later, on a hot, sunshiny morning, a group of housewives came into Ma Procop's yard as she was hanging out the laundry on some makeshift lines between two mango trees. Ma Lambee was not among them, but while they were foregathering she had been telling them exactly what to do.

"Look in she house — I bet you wouldn't see any mirrors. And I bet you, too, that you find a lot of funny things in the house, like bone and bird feather and bottles and one might even find a skeleton."

For Ma Lambee had done what she thought would be the last damning thing — she had sneaked into Ma Procop's hut and hidden all the stuff with which she had been practising her own evil acts, and she had removed the only mirror in the room, and a small crucifix near the head of the bed.

Ma Procop hung out a pair of khaki trousers and turned to face the women. They got to the point right away.

"Ma Procop," the leader said, "we hear that is you who working obeah in the village and causing evil spirit to walk about in the night."

"What nonsense you talking?" she put her hands on her hips and looked outraged.

"Well, anyway, we going to search your house."

They left her standing there and went into the hut. A minute later bottles and bones came hurtling out the window.

"Is true! is true!" the women came tumbling from the hut in fear. "You really working obeah! Look at all these things we find in your room!"

Ma Procop recovered quickly at this unexpected development.

"All these things you see here," she waved her hands to the ground, "they don't belong to me, I swear." She made the sign of the cross with her two forefingers and kissed it loudly. "They belong to Ma Lambee. I sure is she who put them in there, because she so spiteful since I come to the village and take away

all the washing.''

The women began murmuring among themselves. Then suddenly one of them came forward and shoved a mirror in Ma Procop's face.

With a deliberate calm the washer said, ''Thank you,'' and she fixed a piece of coloured cloth she wore on her head, looking straight into the mirror. Then, as if in a rage, she pulled the mirror and dashed it to the ground.

''That is the true test,'' one in the group whispered, ''if she really obeah woman she can't look in a mirror. Ma Lambee must be telling lie! It look as if Ma Procop not guilty!''

Ma Procop caught the turning of the tide. ''Listen,'' she said. ''Let all of us go over by Ma Lambee and give she the test with a mirror and a cross. I have just what we need hide away inside the house, just give me a chance to get it.''

She dashed inside and came back with the parcel she had brought from Donkey City. She took the lead, heading straight for Ma Lambee's hut.

"You Ma Lambee," she shouted as they got into the yard, "you fooling people and saying that is I who working obeah, when is you all the time! Come out here in the yard let we test you!"

Ma Lambee came charging out of the hut. "What you mean by keeping so much noise in my yard?" she demanded. She tried to keep a steady face but she knew that something had gone wrong.

"Look, we have a mirror and a cross here," Ma Procop loosened the parcel and stepped ahead of the group. She moved quickly, and turned the mirror full in Ma Lambee's face, at the same time lifting the cross over her head.

No one heard the strange words Ma Procop was fiercely whispering and the weird glint in her eyes, but everyone saw Ma Lambee cower in fear, and a look of extreme terror come into her face. She began to shake, as if she had ague. Then clasping her hands to her head she turned and ran shrieking into the hut.

Ma Procop turned to the frightened villagers.

"Nothing more to worry about," she said in a tone of authority as she wrapped the mirror and cross into a parcel again. "You will never have any obeah here as long as I stay in the village."

The next morning Ma Procop stood by her hut watching Ma Lambee take the road to Donkey City, all her belongings wrapped in a sheet which she had slung over her shoulder.

As the old woman looked back for a last glimpse of Sans Souci she caught sight of Ma Procop leaning on the fencing, watching her.

With a yell of terror she waddled after her long shadow cast by the morning sun.

from WAYS OF SUNLIGHT

The Day Mama Dot Takes Ill

Fred D'Aguiar

The day Mama Dot takes ill,
The continent has its first natural disaster:
Chickens fall dead on their backs,
But keep on laying rotten eggs; ducks upturn
In ponds, their webbed feet buoyed forever;
Lactating cows drown in their sour milk;
Mountain goats lose their footing on ledges
They used to skip along; crickets croak,
Frogs click, in broad daylight; fruits
Drop green from trees; coconuts kill travellers
Who rest against their longing trunks;
Bees abandon their queens to red ants,
And bury their stings in every moving thing;
And the sun sticks like the hands of a clock
At noon, drying the very milk in breasts.

Mama Dot asks for a drink to quench her feverish
    thirst:
It rains until the land is waist-deep in water.
She dreams of crops being lost: the water drains
In a day leaving them intact. She throws open her
    window
To a chorus and rumpus of animals and birds,
And the people carnival for a week. Still unsteady
On her feet, she hoes the grateful ashes
From the grate and piles the smiling logs on it.

The Peacocks

F. D. Weller

Any time he was out of work and lonely he thought of the peacocks.

When he was a little boy in the country he used to go for a walk with his father every Sunday afternoon, and sometimes they used to walk so far that they would find themselves at last way up in the hills, tired from so much walking but happy, hardly talking, just standing there, letting the cold wind blow on them and feeling the long shadows of evening fall around them. Then on the way back his father would stop at Mrs. Dawkins' big white house at the bottom of the hill and say good evening to old Mrs. Dawkins who was English and very rich but kindhearted. Then he would go with his father and look at Mrs. Dawkins' peacocks.

There were a lot of them. His father used to stand in the near-darkness and make a funny sound with his mouth and the peacocks would scream and run out of the bushes and look at the man and the little boy.

They were very beautiful.

After a while they would get fearful and hide again, then his father would take him by the hand and he would walk slowly home, very sad that the peacocks had left them.

When his father had died his mother had kept bravely at it, and struggled with the little piece of land. He used to try his best to help, but it was too much for a woman and a little boy to manage. Even though Mrs. Dawkins used to send a little something every week for his mother she died at last of overwork and a broken heart. Mrs. Dawkins had arranged for him to come to Kingston and get a job in her brother's shoe factory.

That last evening he had gone to tell her goodbye and thanks, he had walked down to the peacocks to have a last look at them. Standing there he had remembered his father, and looking at their gorgeous tailfeathers he had felt all full and lonely and sad, just like he used to feel every Sunday evening. He had cried there in the dark, by himself. Then he had gone away.

The job at the factory had only lasted for a year. During that time he had come to learn about the city, to know its people and study just what it was that made them different from other people. He thought Kingston was a nice place, if you tried to understand it. And he felt he understood it.

Understanding it was very difficult when you were working and travelling to work on the same bus every morning, seeing the same bored faces, white, black and brown, smelling the same smells while going through the same streets . . . *that* was why one couldn't get to understand Kingston. When he was out of work it was different.

He didn't have to hurry down to work or hurry back home for supper — home usually being some cheap boarding-house. When he wasn't working, like now, and had no money, it was pleasant. He used to get up early in the morning and walk into town. He used to walk down King Street so early he hardly recognised it.

There was no noise and only a few people, and the street looked like a street in a dream, lost and silent, waiting for the people to come and bring it to life again. It would usually be a little before daybreak.

He had nowhere to go, but he'd just walk along all the little lanes and side-streets, breathing deeply because he wasn't in a hurry, looking around him and, it seemed, really seeing the city for the first time. Every place was like a setting on a stage. The public buildings for instance. And the stores.

And the doors and the show-windows, the street-corners and the Cenotaph, and especially the big pale sky over everything.

Things in the windows he could never buy; books, clothes, tennis racquets, footballs, all those things. He would think it terrible that he didn't have a job. It wasn't terrible though.

He didn't come right out and say he hated the idea of a job, being safe and secure and the rest of it. But he hated it.

Sometimes he used to dream about winning the Sweepstake, then he'd give it up because you either had to be a labourer or an iceman or a gravedigger to win the Sweepstake. And he used to hope that he'd get a job and hope that he didn't.

All the time he'd be remembering the peacocks. Their tails, and their funny way of walking and the raucousness of their screams.

Then he'd start thinking about the country and his mother and father and he'd grow sad and fall asleep with his arms around the pillow like a little baby.

This time he was out of work again. But he was sick of walking downtown early in the morning and his money was nearly finished, and soon he only had around five shillings left. At this stage of his unemployment he always indulged in deep philosophical speculation upon the nature of wealth.

He thought money was a funny thing. When you were poor you didn't know about things like lovely houses and delicious meals and going to the theatre twice a week or going for a pleasure cruise to South America or Hawaii.

But when you were rich you lost your sense of how valuable money was, you forget what a good thing a threepence is, you don't know what the world is, what life is, what beauty there is in a cup of coffee when you're hungry . . . or in walking the streets of Kingston before daybreak. They don't know anything at all.

They are afraid, they are perpetually trembling, worrying about taxes and old debts, the government taking away and balancing and levelling off. To them, he reflected, money doesn't mean a thing.

It doesn't mean a thing to me either, he would tell himself defiantly, knowing he was lying, knowing that he wanted another job even though it meant giving up his freedom for a while. Someday, he thought, I'm going to be a millionaire. And he'd turn over and go to sleep again.

All of a sudden he had an irrepressible longing to see those peacocks again. He longed to go back to the country, back in the Clarendon hills. He could feel his youth slipping away from him, he hardly even thought about the peacocks now, but just lay in bed all day staring at the spotty ceiling, thinking, waiting for the slatternly landlady to knock at the door and demand her rent.

He felt he needed a change. Maybe he could go by market class, that wouldn't cost much, then he could go and ask Mrs. Dawkins for something to help him out.

He had stopped writing her for a long time now, ever since he had lost the job for getting in a fight with the boss. He had been ashamed to tell her why, so he had stopped writing her.

And she had stopped sending him money. He hoped she was still alive. And he hoped also that the peacocks were still there. Maybe they were dead now, maybe she was dead . . .

All the way on the train he felt tense and nervous, like a little boy going to school for the first time. He kept looking around him at the people in the carriage, not really seeing them, just trying to connect himself with his surroundings. Outside, the scenery was flying past but he didn't see it. He had a guilty feeling, and he thought of the story of the Prodigal Son.

Suppose Mrs. Dawkins were dead . . . What would he do? Where would he go?

When he came off at the little station no one was there that he remembered. He kept walking through the crowd like he was looking for somebody, peering into people's faces and standing in the dusty little street outside the station, looking up and down. Darkness fell, and he began the long walk out of town. Mrs. Dawkins' place was about seven miles out of town. He hadn't eaten anything the whole way and now he felt hungry.

He walked slowly, letting the cool country air seep into his body and brace him up. All along the road he heard frogs whistling, and far away he heard a dog barking. Every now and then he would meet someone bound in the opposite direction and exchange a hearty "good night" with them, not daring to beg them for a bite of food.

Sometimes he could hardly see where he was going, except for the pale ribbon of the road stretching ahead of him in the darkness. He heard a stream trickling steadily beside the road, but he kept straight on, thinking of the peacocks and remembering those Sunday afternoons.

It would be good to see Mrs. Dawkins again. He wondered if he would ever go back to Kingston. At last he got to the village. It was asleep, and only a couple of mongrels were skulking through the street when he passed. Mrs. Dawkins lived outside the village.

As he turned a bend he saw the big white house sprawling at the foot of the hill. All the lights were off. He walked up the driveway of white marl, scuffing his toes in the powdery material.

Now that he had arrived he felt tired and listless, and he

remembered his hunger again. But he would just have to wait for morning before he could see Mrs. Dawkins. But the peacocks.

He went down behind the house in the dark. It was cold. He felt excited, just as he had felt the first time.

There was the big guinep tree, looking as he remembered it. And the thick croton bushes growing beneath and spreading away back into the commons.

He had to walk carefully because he didn't want the peacocks to get frightened and run away before he saw them. Softly he parted the bushes, making the same sound that his father had made long ago, when he called the peacocks.

Listening to the Land

Martin Carter

That night when I left you on the bridge
I bent down
kneeling on my knee
and pressed my ear to listen to the land.

I bent down
listening to the land
but all I heard was tongueless whispering.

On my right hand was the sea behind the wall
the sea that has no business in the forest
and I bent down
listening to the land
and all I heard was tongueless whispering
as if some buried slave wanted to speak again.

Calypso Finals

Michael Aubertin

Mighty was more than a little apprehensive. He must not fail, not tonight! He had survived the eliminations and they had let him come through the semi-finals with flying colours. He knew it was a trick, just to get him off his guard. Let him feel overconfident and wham! Get him when he least expected it. No, he would not allow them to. They had cheated him out of the crown once too often.

The last three years had been disastrous. The first year, when the mike had started its demented electronic shriek whilst he was in the middle of his best song, he had considered it an accident. He had not been able to recover on that ill–fated night, and his chances were ruined. The following year had seen the first flowering of suspicion in his mind. He had slipped on the stage and the audience had gone into hysterics as he had come crashing down. They were beginning to think he had a jinx, but he knew better. It was obeah! someone had given him a carefully prepared drink before he had gone on stage. It was one of his fellow calypsonians, but in the excitement back stage he had forgotten the culprit. He vowed to be more careful next year. After that show he had confirmed his suspicions. Two calypsonians were in league against him. He distinctly remembered them both slapping him amiably on the back the moment before he went on. The pain that had shot through his fingers, causing him to drop the mike, had been explained as an electric shock. It was not.

And now he was on his guard. He was rated one of the top contenders for the Calypso King title. He must be careful.

He watched the milling crowd and felt a peculiar faintness in the pit of his stomach. First time this place pack like that, he thought. Well, tonight is the night. I going to show them! But how my stomach feeling weak so? Let me take a few deep breaths.

He was in the sixth position, so he had enough time to get used to the audience.

"Singers backstage!" someone whispered in his ear.

Mighty smiled to the calypsonian and moved towards the door. A few of his fans called to him and he waved. Suddenly he felt his right ear ringing and a thought immediately flashed through his mind. He dismissed it, however, because he trusted the calypsonian who had whispered.

The stuffy space behind the screen was crowded with gaudily dressed young men. Costumes hung upon stage props. Everyone was tense. A few calypsonians sipped nervously at the flasks they carried. Mighty went to the farthest corner and settled down. He grinned perfunctorily at those eyes that met his. He must not converse with anyone. They might try to get at him whilst exchanging easy banter.

After a brief fanfare the master of ceremonies gave a dynamic welcome to the audience. Whistles and catcalls came to Mighty's ears and his heart fluttered. The band started to play a tune and the audience sang along.

Not a bad crowd, Mighty thought. They are responding. He looked at the calypsonian who had to open the show. Mighty wondered how he felt. Earlier that evening when they had dipped into the bag to take the slips of paper designating positions, Mighty had prayed not to get the first spot. But perhaps that position would have been better. He would have got it over with sooner. He began to envy the calypsonian.

"And now, we present, the Mighty System!" came the MC's voice. Mighty immediately reappraised the situation and changed his mind. Number six was just fine. Turning to the screen, he put his eyes to the tiny holes and watched the first performer go through his paces. The crowd screamed their acclamation as the first calypsonian came off the stage. Mighty wondered how many points he had scored. The young man came back stage his face flushed with victory.

"How did I do? How did I do?" he demanded.

He was patted on the back by those calypsonians in his camp. The crowd suddenly roared and Mighty felt alarmed. His mind went back to the year he had fallen. He peered through the screen. The MC was entertaining the crowd with a joke.

"I hope tings go alright this year, Mighty," a voice close to him said and Mighty instinctively drew away. It was one of them!

"I-I hope so too," Mighty said, wondering if the calypsonian had touched him.

"I think I going to change a line in my first tune, you know," the other said good-naturedly. He drew an envelope out of his pocket. "Check that for me. I want to know if it rhyming."

Mighty's eyes were rivetted on the envelope. There were words scrawled upon it.

"Hold de ting man!" the other insisted. "Wha happen? Because is competition you ain't going help a pardner?"

Mighty shook his head.

"I too nervous," he dodged. "The mind can't function. Sorry."

He slunk back to his position and slouched in the corner. His heart was thumping. It had been a close call. They miss me, man. They miss me! he thought. Lucky thing I good for myself. If I had hold that envelope!

A burst of applause told him that another singer had finished. How many more to go? He thought. Four. No three. This feller now going on is number three, then number four that's two, then number five, that's three and then number six, that's four. Four? But I'm number six! Just now! He went over the list in his mind again and realised that he was hopelessly confused. He moved to one of the calypsonians.

"You have a programme to lend me?"

"No."

"Who's singing there?"

"Mighty Zando."

"What number?"

"Three."

"Look, how many more to go before me? I'm number six."

"Two more, then you," the calypsonian told him with a strange look.

Two more!? Mighty thought, a dryness spreading to his throat.

"What happen, Mighty?" the calypsonian asked. "You feeling okay?"

"Yeah man," Mighty forced out.

"Well, take it easy, huh?" the other said patting him on the shoulder. Mighty was glad for the sympathy. Not all of them are bad sorts, he thought. The fourth calypsonian sang his two songs without a hitch and then came number five. Mighty went through an agony of suspense. He wished he could prolong the singer's songs forever. Every note which issued out of the musical instruments took Mighty nearer to the time when he would have to face the music. Face the music! he thought. That's a funny one! I have to face the music! An odd sound came out of his throat. Watching himself with a strange detachment, he realised that it was supposed to have been a laugh.

"And now, we present, the Mighty Mighty!"

Mighty faced the glare of the floodlights, winced, and stepped gingerly upon the stage. The applause was deafening. I must not fail them, he thought. They're clapping for me! Self–confidence surged through him.

"Good evening ladies and gentlemen," he said into the mike. There he thought. I didn't say goodnight. I said good evening. I bet the other fellers said goodnight.

"Lewee go!" he ordered, and the rhythmic strains of his music filled the hall. He responded like the born calypsonian that he was. He teased and coaxed his audience into a frenzy. He was in command. The buggers miss me, he thought, as he ended his

first song. I have them this year. I have them! He glanced to his
right and saw a few faces peeking out of the back stage door.
They were beaming. He felt like laughing. Why had he been so
needlessly afraid? The next song was his favourite.

"Strike up de band!" he hurled and went into his next song.
He negotiated the first verse and a chorus and watched the
audience go wild with delight. They love me, he thought. They
love me! I is the king this year! The band played on, gave him his
cue, and he melted into the second verse of the song. The chorus
done, he appraised the audience once more. These people really
enjoying this song, he thought, feeling fortunate that he had
thought of the idea first. Suddenly he realised that he did not
know what verse was to be sung next. Cool it boy, cool it! he told
himself anxiously. You've sung two verses. It's verse three now.
How does it go again? How does it go again!? He panicked as he
came to the realisation that his mind was as blank as a newborn
baby's. The band moved inexorably to the end of their strain,
when they would give him his cue. He glanced to his right in
consternation, and saw a certain calypsonian smiling at him. They
got me! he thought. The buggers got me! and he plunged
inevitably into the beginning of the very verse he had just sung.

South Parade Peddler

Louise Bennett

Hairnet! Scissors! Fine-teet comb!
– Whe de nice lady deh?
Buy a scissors from me, no, lady?
Hair pin? Tootpase? Go weh!
Me seh go-weh aready, ef
Yuh doan like it, see me.
Yuh dah swell like bombin plane fun —
Yuh soon bus up like Graf Spee.

Yuh favour — Shoeslace! Powder puff!
Clothes hanger! Belt! Pen knife!
Buy someting, no, nice young man?
Buy a hairnet fi yuh wife.
Buy someting wid de change, no, sah,
An meck de Lawd bless yuh!
Me no sell farden hair curler, sah!
Yuh fas an facety to!

Teck yuh han outa me box!
Pudung me razor blade!
Yuh no got no use fi it, for yuh
Dah suffer from hair raid!
Nice boonoonoonoos lady, come,
Me precious, come dis way.
Hair pin? Yes, mah, tank yuh, yuh is
De bes one fi de day.

Toot-brush? Ah beg yuh pardon, sah —
Me never see yuh mout:
Dem torpedo yuh teet, sah, or
Yuh female lick dem out?
No bodder pick me up, yaw, sah!
Yuh face look like a seh
Yuh draw it outa lucky box.
No bodder me — go weh!

One police man dah come, but me
Dah try get one more sale.
Shoeslace! Tootpase! Buy quick, no, sah!
Yuh waan me go a jail?
Ef dah police ever ketch we, Lize,
We peddler career done.
Pick up yuh foot eena yuh han.
Hair pin! Hair curler! Run!

Supermarket Blues

Hazel Campbell

Miss Maud was going to the shop; the Three Tees Supermarket to be more exact. She settled the slightly dirty white hat which had been down-graded from dress-up church-hat to street-hat over her thick grey plaits; wiped her face with her hands still greasy from plaiting her hair, and looked around for the plastic bag she always carried with her when shopping.

She lifted her hat once more to place the change purse under it before leaving her room. She had started doing that since the thinness of her body coupled with age caused her to have no more use for a brassiere. Since there was nothing to retain the change purse in her bosom, she now wore it under her hat.

In the supermarket she would find a corner, turn her back and, with what she hoped were unnoticeable movements, fish out the purse from under the hat before going to the counter to pay for her goods.

Since she usually didn't take a trolley for the few things she wanted, and walked with the groceries piled in her hands or in a box, getting at the purse was often a complicated exercise. Sometimes she forgot to get the purse before checking the goods and then she had to feel for it right before everybody's eyes. She didn't mind their seeing her; what she was afraid of was that they would follow her and try to steal her money. She wasn't sure who "they" were but there were so many stories about thieves these days she couldn't help being afraid.

But she need not have worried. Her generally shabby appearance together with the few groceries she purchased would never lead anyone to suspect that she had money worth stealing. In fact she didn't.

Her daughter in America owned the house she lived in along with some eight other tenants. She didn't pay any rent. A regular $20 a month, an occasional sum from her son in England, occasional gifts of food from her relatives in the country and a Christmas box from the States kept her alive.

She was grateful for this. Indeed she was better off than some of the other tenants in the yard. Especially the young women with small children. Often it was she to whom the children came for a midday meal of porridge and crackers while their mothers were out "looking work."

Miss Maud shut her door and walked toward the gate. Before she could reach it, two voices called out to her.

"Buy some sugar fe me no?"

"Wait little, Miss Maud, ef you see any condense milk, buy two tin fe me."

"Ef me see any," she answered, waiting while the two women brought her the money to make their purchases.

"Ef me se any," Miss Maud repeated aloud as she waited to cross the busy main road before the Three Tees Plaza. Of late she had started talking to herself a lot.

"After them no have nutten inna the shop dem again. Las week me no get no soap powder. Me have fe buy new fangle water soap whey me no like. Me no get no flour neither. Wonder what them no have this week," she sighed.

Since the shortages started, the rows of empty shelves testifying to the absence of many needed items, Miss Maud had fallen into the habit of haunting the two supermarkets near to her every day. Since she didn't have to take a bus and didn't mind the exercise, every morning at about ten o'clock she visited one or the other, sometimes both, in the hope of finding the scarce items.

If she was lucky she might be on spot when the two or three cartons of soap powder were opened and then she would get one. Also if she waited long enough, and begged hard enough, one of the men who packed goods in the back room might take pity on her and bring out a tin of milk or a pack of chicken necks and backs or a pack of sugar depending on what was short.

Sometimes too, she had to beg them to package a smaller amount of cornmeal or flour because the packs on the shelves had more than she could pay for or carry comfortably.

"Life get so hard," Miss Maud continued her soliloquy. "It bad enough that the little money can't stretch, but even when you have it, sometimes you can't get nutten fi buy."

Sixty-six years old, lonely because all her children had gone away, confused by the many rapid changes around her, Miss Maud hurried across the road when the light showed the green "walk" signal.

She arrived on the other side a little breathless, straightened her hat and turned into the Three Tees Plaza.

The supermarket door flew open as she stepped on the mat making her heart flutter a little. No matter how often she came to the supermarket, the magic door which flew open without a touch always managed to surprise her.

She entered the large store and smiled at the young packer who was standing idly by, leaning against one of the take-out trolleys.

"Morning, son," she greeted him. "How tings today eh?"

"Same as usual, Granny," he replied and turned away. He didn't want to get into conversation with her. The other packers teased him because he was polite to the customers and the older women especially liked to stop and chat with him.

As she passed through the turnstile Miss Maud noticed that there weren't many people in the store. It was the time when she best liked to shop. When there were too many people in the store pushing and shoving to get things from the shelves she got confused and sometimes forgot what she wanted. And she never forgot the time, months before, how she was nearly trampled in the rush for rice when a few packs were brought out. They had had to close the supermarket and call the police. Since then she had grown afraid of crowds. When the store was empty she could take her time and if she forgot anything she could look around until she remembered what it was she wanted.

As she hesitated by the turnstile wondering as she always did whether to take a trolley, a handbasket, or simply keep the things in her hands, a woman brushed past her with an impatient "excuse me."

Mrs. Telfer was in a bad mood. She was late for work again. Because of the shortages she too had taken to haunting the supermarkets, three or four of them, three or four times each week, in the hope of filling her grocery needs. What one shop didn't have she sometimes found in another. And, of course, being on good terms with more than one manager meant that she would get three packs of soap and so on, one from each, depending on which item was short.

But it took up so much time! She was having to sneak out from work at odd times during the day or go in late with some inadequate excuse. Of late her boss had been staring at her whenever she went in late. He hadn't said anything yet but she was sure that it was just a matter of time.

She wasn't happy about the situation, but what could she do? she asked herself. She didn't mind the shortages. Food didn't bother her. She could do without many of the things she had to hunt and scrounge for, but her husband and her two sons were forever complaining when she told them that the things they liked just weren't available.

"I don't like this soap. It stinks! Why did you buy it?" her husband would ask.

She would patiently explain that it was the only brand available.

"You just write your sister in Chicago or John and tell them to send you some decent soap," he would command her. "Is better you don't bathe than use this. You smell stinker after you use it," and he would bang the bathroom door to emphasise his annoyance.

"Mummy, you sure them don't have no Kellogs?" her elder son would wail, both elbows on the table, leaning over the porridge he didn't want.

"No, Joseph," she would patiently explain for the millionth time. "There's no Kellogs. Eat your porridge before your father leave you again this morning."

"I don't like this black sugar," the little one would then begin. "It don't taste good."

They nagged her as if all these changes were her fault. As if she could manufacture the things they wanted, the things they

69

had been accustomed to, out of thin air.

If Three Tees manager couldn't find a bottle of coffee for her today she was sure she would have to move out of the house, she thought. She couldn't face that miserable man in the morning and tell him that there was no coffee. She wondered with brief humour who she could sue for breaking up her marriage.

Not the government, she was sure. They said it wasn't their fault.

Mrs. Telfer put her handbag in the trolley and pushed it briskly before her.

Miss Maud was taking her time about her shopping. She looked at the tightly squeezed-up dollar notes in her hand and tried to remember what her neighbours had asked her to buy. "Tilda want sugar and milk. Valda want soap and milk too," she said aloud, moving around to look for the groceries. A little commotion at the entrance caused her to look back.

A large woman, fat and sweating, had entered with her small child and was teasing the shy packer.

"Morning, George," she greeted him loudly, much to the amusement of the others.

"You leave anything for me today?"

"Wha him have, yu no want it!" one of the grinning youths told her.

"Who sey me no want it?" she laughed. "When you gwine gi me? Enh, Mr. George?" she teased the youth who was busy trying not to look as uncomfortable as he felt.

"Him ketch fraid. Him can't manage you," another one said.

"Cho! Me fat but me easy fi manage," the woman said, still laughing. Then suddenly she stopped laughing and said in a stern voice, "Me want some chicken back and flour this morning an oonu better no tell me no foolishness say oonu no have none!" she announced loudly to the shop at large. The two cashiers who didn't yet have very much to do looked at each other and raised their eyebrows at the fat woman's behaviour.

It didn't take Miss Maud very long to pick up the few things she wanted. She had found milk but looked in vain for onions. The food just didn't taste the same without the onions. And she couldn't afford to pay the price they were asking on the plaza.

Furthermore they had married it to yam or something else.

She had been lucky to catch the eye of one of the storeroom packers and had begged him to bring some sugar and a few onions for her. She was willing to pay the 80c or so they would cost and do without something else this week.

She waited almost ten minutes before the packer returned with only one pack of sugar. "But is two me beg you," she protested. "Them gal a yard beg me buy fi them."

"Oonu gwine have fi share that," the man answered rudely. "No more no pack," he said and shut the door in her face.

"Wha 'bout onion?" she asked the door.

Sighing wearily Miss Maud walked towards the cashier to pay for the groceries.

Mrs. Telfer was looking at her half-full trolley in disgust. Most of the things she had picked up she didn't need — at least not yet, since she had some at home. But it had become a habit with her not to pass up items which might become short in the future. It wasn't that she meant to hoard. But take toilet paper for instance. One month ago they had been reduced to the last roll at home. She had had to buy box tissues to fill the family's needs, and endure a number of often downright rude remarks from her husband. Now she automatically picked up an extra roll or two everytime she shopped.

This little shopping spree would cause her to overspend her budget again for the week, she knew, but she had almost given up the 'battle of the balancing budget' as she and her friends called it. So it really didn't matter. She would ask Ralph for more money and he would shout at her, yelling that she was asking for more and more money and bringing less and less into the house.

Men never understood, Mrs. Telfer sighed. He would talk for hours about the economic situation of the country, balance of payments problems, explain to his bewildered friends that the bad planning in the past had brought the country to its present situation, but ask him to use newspaper instead of toilet paper as she had once suggested! Mrs. Telfer could smile now as she remembered his comment on that suggestion. And as to his whisky! He still managed to make sure that he had at least one bottle in the house.

Her only consolation this morning was that the manager had given her a bottle of coffee, discreetly wrapped with the price marked on the paper bag so that the cashier could check it without even knowing what was inside. But he had given her no oil.

Somewhere in the supermarket she could hear a woman's voice boisterously abusing somebody for not giving her any oil. The voice was tracing the other person's ancestry back to monkey days in the forest. The people who behaved like that usually got what they wanted Mrs. Telfer thought. But she would have to starve before anybody got her to do that.

A little way from the cashier she paused to check her purse for money. She always did this since the day she had suffered the acute embarrassment of not having any money to pay the cashier after the goods had already been checked.

Miss Maud had also stopped to worry about the second pack of sugar which she hadn't got. She was wondering what was the best thing for her to do. Maybe Little Corner Supermarket would have, she thought. She sorted out the money to pay for the different goods and satisfied that she had it correct she began to move toward the cashier just as Mrs. Telfer started to push her trolley forward. Seeing Mrs. Telfer's half-full trolley, Miss Maud with her few items hastened to get in front of her. In her hurry she didn't notice the jutting back wheel of Mrs. Telfer's trolley not until she tripped over it, and to the horror of all the onlookers, banged her head on the side of it as she fell to the floor.

Tins of milk, box of soap, pack of sugar — all the things she had been clutching — flew in all directions and as she struggled to pull herself up on hands and knees, blood began to drip slowly onto the floor.

The supermarket froze, as if the dripping blood had mesmerised them all. Nobody moved. Not the cashier who had been getting ready to receive the goods; not George the young packer with whom she had smiled when she entered the store; not the manager who had been passing just then; not the idle packers congregating by the door; and certainly not Mrs. Telfer.

With horror, Mrs. Telfer watched the drops of blood pooling and the old woman kneeling, unable to rise. Somewhere in Mrs.

Telfer's head was the thought that she should move, should help the old woman to her feet, find out how badly hurt she was. Something in the way the old woman looked reminded her of her own Aunt Jo and her heart turned over in sympathy. And still she did not move.

She wanted to reach out and hug the bleeding head. She wanted to comfort the old woman who had started to moan, but even later when she was telling the story she couldn't explain why she never moved.

Suddenly the fat boisterous woman, coming it seemed from nowhere, burst around the corner. Hurrying to Miss Maud, she roughly pushed Mrs. Telfer's trolley out of the way and gently lifted the old woman off the floor. She helped her to stand up and grabbed a pack of toilet paper from Mrs. Telfer's shopping.

Breaking open the pack she took out a roll and tore off a piece which she used to wipe the blood which was trickling down the old woman's face.

"Them can't charge we fi this," she said, tearing off more and more paper.

"Come Granny. Look how you mash up you face this big big Tuesday morning. Come we go outside in the fresh air mek me see how it stay."

"Jilly!" she called to the small child who had come shopping with her. "Tek up Granny hat and her purse and beg them a bottle, ketch little cold water at the cooler.

"Hurry!" she ordered and kept up a constant chatter, bemoaning the old woman's wound and threatening punishment against the management as she led Miss Maud outside.

With a sigh of relief the supermarket thawed.

"All right," the manager shouted. "One of you idle boy get a mop and clean up this mess. Move it!"

George went to find a container to get the little child the water.

The cashier settled herself on her chair and began to punch her machine as Mrs. Telfer unloaded her trolley. Mrs. Telfer's brown face had turned very pale, as if it was she who had lost the blood now drying on the floor.

"I'll pay for the paper," she almost whispered to the cashier who didn't reply.

Jamaica Market

Agnes Maxwell-Hall

Honey, pepper, leaf-green limes,
Pagan fruit whose names are rhymes,
Mangoes, breadfruit, ginger-roots,
Granadillas, bamboo-shoots,
Cho-cho, ackees, tangerines,
Lemons, purple Congo-beans,
Sugar, akras, kola-nuts,
Citrons, hairy coconuts,
Fish, tobacco, native hats,
Gold bananas, woven mats,
Plantains, wild-thyme, pallid leeks,
Pigeons with their scarlet beaks,
Oranges and saffron yams,
Baskets, ruby guava jams,
Turtles, goat-skins, cinnamon,
Allspice, conch-shells, golden rum.
Black skins, babel — and the sun
That burns all colours into one.

Childhood

Grace Nichols

My childhood
was a watershed of sunlight
and strange recurring mysteries

the fishes before a drought
came in droves
floundering at our backdoors

saltwater drove them in
moving groggy shadows
beneath the mirror surfacing

sunfish/patwa/butterfish
half stunned I watched
bare hand I gripped

at Sunday school
we didn't learn to pray
for the dying freshwater souls of fish

Sharlo's Strange Bargain

Ralph Prince

In Glentis Village, when people notice that you love your belly, they often say: "You belly goin' bring you to de same en' like Sharlo." And then they would tell you the story of Sharlo and his strange bargain. It's an old, old story, and they say it's true. This is how it goes:

There once lived a man in Glentis Village named Sharlo. Some called him "Long-belly Sharlo", because he loved food too much. Others called him "Sharlo the Fifer", because he was the best fife player in the village. The fife was made from bamboo in Sharlo's own secret way, and it was the sweetest fife the villagers had ever heard. They believed that the music he played on it was the sweetest in all the world.

One afternoon Sharlo was returning home after working in his lands in the mountain. He was on the lower slopes, but still a long way from home, when a heavy shower of rain began to fall. He sheltered under a tree, but he got slightly wet all the time. The rain poured in torrents all afternoon and evening, enveloping the mountain in a thick, white sheet.

When darkness gathered, Sharlo felt cold and miserable. So he took out his fife and played it. He played all the old songs he could remember — songs of the old folk when they lived in the mountain, songs of the fishermen in Glentis Village, sad songs and merry songs. All these and more he played and played, sweeter than he had ever played before.

Then suddenly he stopped playing. Right before him appeared a tall, red man. Sharlo was astonished, for he had not seen where the man had come from. "Go ahead playing," said the man. "You played so sweet that I came up from down yonder to hear you."

Sharlo asked him who he was, and the man said that everybody knew him. Sharlo then looked at him closely to see if he really knew him. The man seemed neither young nor old, but ageless. His skin was red and looked like the shell of a boiled lobster. His hair was white and flowing. His eyes were red, and

they glowed as if fires burned within them. "Never see you
before," said Sharlo, after looking at him searchingly and long.

"You will soon remember who I am," declared the man, "and
you will get to know me more, Sharlo."

"How you know me name?" asked Sharlo, in surprise.

"Aha!" laughed the man. "I know everybody, Sharlo —
everybody in this world!"

Meanwhile Sharlo was still getting wet, so he edged up closer to the trunk of the tree. But the rain ran off the man's body like water sliding off a duck's back.

"Would you like to come down to my place for shelter?" asked the man.

Sharlo wondered where that place was. But he was wet, and above all, hungry, so he agreed to go, hoping to get some food there. The man led the way and Sharlo followed. As fast as the man walked, a hole opened in the mountain before him, going downwards all the time.

At last he stopped. Sharlo found himself in a large, oven-like room with fires burning along the walls. It was so hot that his clothes soon became dry and he had to take off his shirt; but the man was not even sweating.

He offered Sharlo a chair before a table, and then sat facing Sharlo. The man said nothing, but watched him intently. Sharlo yawned several times, expecting the man to offer him something to eat. But the man just watched him intently and said nothing. At last Sharlo could bear it no longer. "You got any food?" he asked.

"Plenty," the man replied. "I was waiting for you to ask for some." He then put a large, empty calabash on the table before Sharlo.

"What would you like to eat?" asked the man, smiling.

"Anyt'ing," answered Sharlo.

"Just say what you want," the man explained, "and this magic calabash will give it you. But you must say it in rhyme, like this:

Calabash, calabash, food time come;
Bring, bring pepperpot an' gee me some."

And so Sharlo did as the man said, and repeated the rhyme:

"Calabash, calabash, food time come;
Bring, bring pepperpot an' gee me some."

And then like magic, hot pepperpot instantly sprang up in the calabash, filling it to the brim. Sharlo was amazed. His eyes bulged. But already his mouth was watering.

"Have a bellyful," said the man. "Eat your pepperpot — it's yours, all yours." So Sharlo ate and ate, until his stomach was full and the calabash was empty. Then he licked his fingers.

The man then asked Sharlo to play the fife for him. As his stomach was full, Sharlo played even sweeter than before.

"You play wonderfully," said the man, smiling. "I wish I could play as sweet as you." And he borrowed the fife and played a tune. To Sharlo's surprise the man played beautifully, though not half as sweet as he.

"A wonderful fife you have here," said the man, rubbing his hand over the keys. "Mmmm hmmm. A wonderful fife."

But Sharlo was hardly listening. He was gazing at the calabash and imagining how wonderful it would be if he could have one like it, to give him all the food he wanted.

"You seem to like the calabash, Sharlo," the man remarked.

Sharlo smiled.

"Would you like to have it?" asked the man.

Sharlo smiled again.

"Very well," said the man, "then we can make a bargain."

"A bargain?" asked Sharlo, in surprise.

"Yes," replied the man, rubbing his hand over the keys of the fife, "a bargain that we must keep secret."

"Wha' is de bargain?" asked Sharlo.

"You take my calabash," the man explained, "and I take your fife."

Sharlo considered the matter for a while. He wanted the calabash, but he didn't want to part with his fife. He had had it since he was young. It was the best fife in the village. And playing it was his greatest joy — next to eating. He hesitated, unable to make up his mind.

"Come, Sharlo," said the man, "be sensible. You can always get another fife, but never another calabash like this again."

"Even in hard times," the man went on, "this magic calabash will give you all the food you want. Think of the fungee and saltfish; the dumplings and pork; the rice and meat; the pepperpot; the souse; the ackee — all these and more are yours, all yours, just for the asking — and the eating."

These were the very dishes Sharlo loved most. And with the calabash so near, the temptation was too great.

"All right," he said at last, "gimme de calabash an' tek de fife." And so the man gave Sharlo the calabash and kept the fife.

He then led Sharlo back up the hole. The rain was over. "Mind you, Sharlo!" said the man as they shook hands, "keep our bargain a secret — otherwise it will be hell with me and you." Sharlo promised to keep the bargain a secret, and they parted.

As he walked home Sharlo wondered who the strange man was. But he soon dropped the matter from his mind as he thought of the magic calabash he had got all for himself. And to test it again he said:

"Calabash, calabash, food time come;
Bring, bring ackee an' gee me some.'

And he ate the ackee all the way home.

From then onwards the calabash provided Sharlo with all the food he fancied. But from that same time he stopped cultivating his mountain lands or doing any other work. He did not get another fife, for he did not love music any more. All he now lived for was to eat.

So as the weeks passed he waxed fatter and fatter, and he became bigger than anyone else in Glentis Village. His face was round like the dumplings he ate every day, and it became so fat that he could barely open his eyes. His body took on a barrel-like bulge, and his belly sagged over his belt like that of a pig hanging down. Six months went by, and life for Sharlo went on like this — no work, no music, and food in abundance whenever he wanted.

Then hard times struck the island. There came a long drought and life became hard for the people of Glentis Village. Many of them starved, and sometimes their only food was sugar-cane. But Sharlo's magic calabash continued to give him all he wanted. He ate more than ever, sometimes feasting like a king.

Then suddenly his dream of endless feasting ended. It happened this way. The drought had been on for three months and the villagers began to wonder where Sharlo was getting food from. For he did not go to the shops to buy anything. And his neighbours did not see him cook anything. So when he walked down the road people sometimes asked: "But Sharlo, how you doin' so well an' we ketchin so much hell?"

This always made him laugh. And as he laughed his eyes would close, and his many chins would tremble and his belly would shake like that of a pig when it runs. But all he would say was: "Shut-mout' no ketch fly."

So the source of his food supply remained a mystery, even to his best friends. An old friend of his named Zakky was constantly trying to find out, but Sharlo would not tell. All he would say was: "Shut-mout' no ketch fly."

But as the drought wore on, Zakky became desperate, for he had a wife and ten children to feed. One evening he went to see Sharlo. Sharlo was finishing a calabash of calaloo. He swallowed the last mouthful, rumbled a belch, licked his fingers, stretched his legs across the floor, and peered out of his fat, fleshy eyes at Zakky.

"Ay Sharlo," Zakky called out, "wha' do?"

"Ah bwoy," Sharlo replied, "me dey — jus' a-mek out."

"Man you nah mekkin out," Zakky declared, "you fat like mud."

Sharlo rumbled another belch and laughed as he clasped his fat hands across his barrel of a stomach. Zakky gazed hard at the calabash for a while and then said: "But Sharlo, man you wort'less."

"Wha' me do?" asked Sharlo.

"Man, you wort'less," Zakky repeated. "You know me an' me wife an' ten pickny an' dem a-dead fo' hungry, an' you never one time say, 'Here Zakky, tek dis food fo' all-you nyam'!"

"Me food too poor fo' you," said Sharlo.

"Too poor!" cried Zakky, "an' de calaloo you jus' done nyam smell so nice? Man, me could nyam da calabash full o' calaloo clean right now!"

Sharlo gazed at Zakky's thin body and bony face and hollow eyes, and felt sorry for him. "All right Zakky," he said, "ah givin' you some food, but you mustn' tell anybody 'bout it." He then recited the magic rhyme:

"Calabash, calabash, food time come;
Bring, bring calaloo an' gee me some."

Immediately the calabash became filled to the brim with hot calaloo. Zakky was amazed. He stared at the calabash with bulging eyes. At last he said, "Well, well, well! So dis is how you gettin' food — by obeah!"

"Is not obeah," Sharlo replied.

"Is by obeah!" Zakky repeated. "So you become a big obeah man, eh Sharlo?"

"Is not obeah," Sharlo repeated in defence. "Zakky, ah tell you is not obeah." Sharlo was afraid that Zakky would spread the word around, because it was an awful thing in Glentis Village to be called an obeah man.

"Well, if is not obeah," said Zakky, "wha' it is eh? Tell me, Sharlo, how else you get dis calabash full o' calaloo but by obeah?"

"All right, Zakky," replied Sharlo, "ah will tell you, but you mus' keep it a secret. Go ahead eat de calaloo, is good food; ah goin' tell you de story."

Zakky began to eat the calaloo, and as he ate, Sharlo told him the whole story. When he mentioned the tall, red man, Zakky laughed. After a while he laughed so much that he had to stop eating. By the time Sharlo had finished his story, Zakky was rocking with uncontrollable laughter, holding his sides as if they were bursting.

"Wha' mek you laugh so?" asked Sharlo.

"Is de bargain you mek wid de devil," Zakky replied.

"De devil!" cried Sharlo, in surprise.

Zakky then explained that the tall, red man who appeared suddenly as from nowhere, and who lived in that hot place down below, and who had provided such a magic calabash, could have been no one else but the devil. It was only then that it slowly dawned on Sharlo that the man he had made the bargain with was indeed the devil.

Sharlo had always heard that it was not wise to deal with the devil, and he began to imagine what the devil had meant when he said it would be hell if the bargain was not kept a secret. He became fearful, and shuddered. He begged Zakky again and again not to tell anyone about the bargain.

Zakky promised to keep the secret. And to encourage him, Sharlo repeated the magic rhyme several times and filled a bucket of food for him to take home, and told him to return any time for more

The next morning Zakky and his wife and their ten children went to Sharlo's home with the empty bucket for more food. They met the house open, with the front door broken off.

"Sharlo!" Zakky called.

No answer came.

Zakky and his wife and their ten children went inside.

"Sharlo!" Zakky called again, "a whey you? A whey de calabash?"

No answer came.

They searched all over the house, and outside in the yard, and everywhere in Glentis Village, but neither Sharlo nor the calabash was anywhere to be seen.

The villagers searched for him for a long time, even in his mountain lands. But Sharlo was never seen again.

Spring

John Robert Lee

come, kneel
scratch, scrape
dig here
with your hands.
beneath this dry ground
is fresh water.

Labourer
man of the earth
teach me the divining certainty within your palms
that I may even now plunge down soft hands
into this heart of dirt and stone
to cup them firmly full around the darkening roots of soil:

rusting cans, coal ashes used to cover over planted seeds
dry antfull sticks that once held up fine pigeon peas
and young tomato plants

dig again with dirty finger nails
throw up and out and far away those quivering fleshless worms
that shift here:

down again down
down past seasons of old yams and sweet potato
down where the fowls cannot go down

dig
dig
dig down into this furrowed flesh
and with the rising sun's firm hoe
make grace upon this turned up earth.

Is this water
on my hands?

wash
drink
give thanks.

Only One Blow of the Wind

John Hearne

We stayed for a little while, looking down the precipice to the rocks at the bottom; then as we turned to go back to the Gap, I knew what it was that had troubled me during the night and this morning. It had gathered far down in the east while we were chasing the hog. A dull, angry-looking copper bruise that had completely overlaid the pale bright blue. It was this and the hot carved stillness around us that suddenly became a memory and a warning in my mind. I went up to Carl quickly. There was really no need for haste. I had left it too late.

"We'll have to move," I said. "There's a hurricane coming. I don't think we'll make it to the Pen in time, but we'll have to try."

His eyes followed to where I was looking. The others looked, too. They all saw it then. I had seen it first because Fabricus Head was on the east coast and in the old days I had been able to watch the hurricanes coming in across the water. They began far out, near Africa, and came across the Atlantic and we had always got them first on the coast. We had got them first and worse than anyone else.

"You're right," Carl said. "How long d'you think we have?"

"I don't know. A few hours. They must have started giving the warnings last night some time."

"You think we'll get back to the Pen before it?"

"No, but we just might."

"What a hell of a thing, eh? We haven't had one in twenty years."

"Nineteen," I said. "We had one the year before we left the Head."

"Let's go. Sheila's never seen a hurricane before. It's no time for her to face one alone."

"Don't worry, Carl," Oliver said. "Sybil will know what to do."

We were going back across the razor-back as we talked. We were in single file, with Graham and Jojo in front setting a jog-pace.

We were more than half-way to the Pen before I told them that we ought to stop. We had come down from the Gap very fast, with Ferdie riding behind each of us in turn. This was late in the afternoon, almost dark. The sky was streaky and brown; it had become grubbier with every hour that we rode. The air felt as if you were being stuffed under hot blankets and the leaves were absolutely still. When you listened it felt strange, and you realized this was because you weren't hearing any insects but only the water down the hillsides. The dogs were ahead. They ran swiftly, with their heads low, and they didn't snap among themselves.

"We'll have to stop here," I said loudly and pulled on the reins.

"No," Carl said. "Let's go on. It'll be less to cover back to the Pen afterwards." His big face was pinched and tight with anxiety.

"If we don't stop here," I said, "we'll get caught in the valley and be washed away for sure."

"Listen to him, Mass' Carl," John Graham said. "Him know what him say." He had turned his mule across the little trail.

Jojo and Oliver didn't say anything. Carl looked at them and they nodded to Graham and me.

"Turn the beasts loose," I said, "and let's dig in. Hurry, eh. We don't have much time." We were high up on the shoulder of a hill. It was grassy and smooth and there was another hill behind us that would break the full wind. There was nowhere else that we could go. When we got from the mules and began to dig a shelf out of the hillside with the machetes, the beasts wouldn't move. They stayed close, and the dogs lay flat along the ground and never took their eyes from us.

We dug a narrow shelf into the hillside. It was like a trench except that the sides were one above the other. The ground sloped before us down to a river. There was a large grove of trees behind us on the left. When we all got into the trench with the dogs it was unbearably hot. The mules stayed near. We had taken the rifles and shot-guns from them, and the three bottles of rum. There wasn't room for anything else in the trench. I didn't think we would have to wait long. While we were waiting I scrambled out and went to my mule and took my plastic wash-bag from the saddle-bag and put my cigarettes into the waterproof plastic. I went back into the trench and held the bag open for the other packets of cigarettes. The mule tried to push its head into the trench and we had to slap the coarse, bony face before it would go away. We were all listening and watching the still leaves on the trees across the river. It was almost night and we could just see the leaf spray of the branches.

"Here it is," I said and watched the branches dip and shiver and the long grass ruffle. It was bent delicately for half a second and then went flat and ugly as the wind leapt over the hill with a solid, roaring scream. The rain came before the wind; a scatter of big drops first, and then a thick almost horizontal wall of grey. Just before the water shuttered everything from sight, we saw a big cinchona bounce madly, root over branch, down the hillside.

The hill was quivering like a big animal and one of the dogs had its head inside my shirt. For about five minutes after the rain there was a peculiar light, half-grey, half-luminous. Then it was dark. It was too dark to see anything at all; and the only sounds were the screaming, steady bellow of the wind and the pounding of the rain on the hillside. The trench was wet and it had become suddenly cool. I was between Oliver and Ferdie.

It went on for five hours. At first it didn't seem possible that the wind could keep to that unrelaxing, unvarying shriek. But it did. We were very cold and the floor of the little dug-out was muddy and chill. Water as it ran down the hillside poured in a sheet across the entrance of the dug-out. The wind and the rain were too loud for us to distinguish other noises plainly, but sometimes there was the deep clang of thunder coming through the sound they made. Sometimes, too, there was a confused ripping crash. When my teeth began to chatter, I took the bottle of rum from inside my shirt and passed it to Ferdie beside me. He drank and gave the bottle to his father. After Carl had taken some they passed it back to me and I handed it to Oliver for him and Jojo. I was glad when it was my turn. The spirit caught keenly in my throat and the glow of its head began before it was in my stomach.

Then the wind began to lull. It was still strong, but without that high deadly scream, and we could hear the fast, deep roar of the river below us. The rain still drove loudly before the wind. I felt Jojo shake me hard, reaching across Oliver to do it.

"Come here!" he bawled. I could hardly catch the words, even in the little box we had dug. He sounded serious.

I crawled over Oliver, squeezing between him and the earth above. Jojo took my hand and thrust it into the darkness outside. The water pouring across the entrance was cold and the driven rain stung my flesh.

"Feel that!" he bellowed close in my ear and pushed my hand into a very fast rush of water. I felt around outside the entrance and up the hillside behind our trench, as far as my arm would go. All I could feel was the deep, thick race of water. Jojo shone his torch beside me and I saw the rain in the beam and then the crumpled, shiny surface of the water where a new channel had been scooped into the hillside. The water was very fast and it was coming down the hill just beside our trench and across the slope before the entrance. There was only a narrow strip of safe land left, over on Carl's side. The surface of the water was very near to the entrance and when I plunged my arm in, I couldn't touch the bottom.

"Let's get out of here!" I shouted to Jojo. I was very frightened and wondered how long we had before the gully race washed our dug-out into the river. He nodded, and I crawled back quickly and shouted to Graham and Carl.

"Mind the wind doesn't blow you in!" I yelled as Carl began to crawl out of the trench. In the torch-beam I could see him pressed flat and digging his fingers into the ground as he wriggled out and up. The low bank of the channel looked very near. Graham and Ferdie went next. The man crawled with his body between the wind and his son; the boy had one arm tight round his father's neck and his free arm thrust sideways and stiff, the fingers dug into the earth. Carl helped them up beside him. I put the torch back into my pocket and poked my head out. The wind caught me and I began to skid helplessly, tumbling sideways towards the water. I sank my fingers up to their knuckles in the rain-soft ground and pressed into the mud. Then I felt Graham's enormous hand close on my wrist, and the light from Carl's torch shone in my face. There was a noise between howling and hissing in the night around me. As I scrambled up beside the other two, a huge rain-drop, hurtling on the wind, hit me in the eyeball. It hurt like the stone from a catapult. Lying flat on the hillside above the tumbling water in the new gully was not hard. The wind kept pushing under us but it was safe enough. I joined my torch to Carl's, and in the grey, packed lines of rain I saw Oliver's head and shoulders come out from the trench. The wind rolled him as he came out and Graham reached down and grabbed his wrist. Between them they began to drag him up beside us. I was shining my light on the wrist Graham held and I could see Oliver's thin small hand sprouting from the other man's huge, flat one. Then I saw the hand vanishing into the fist and felt Graham lunge forward beside me and lifting the beam up I caught Oliver's white face among the rain as the wind hit him square and pushed him into the darkness where the gully was. I saw this, and in the same instant heard Jojo's bellow of, "Oliver!" burst through the howling wind; and saw the quick blur of his body against the rain-dimmed beam of the torch as he dived from the dug-out into the water.

Carl, Graham, Ferdie and I spent the rest of the night up the hillside, under the grove of trees. None of them had blown down and with the wind dropping it was the safest place to be until day-light. We had left the dogs to follow if they could, but they hadn't come after us as we crawled up the hill in the mud and flattened grass. I had no feeling inside me, except a numb disbelief. The two bodies going into the water seemed like many years ago; in another country.

"How am I supposed to tell Sybil?" I asked Carl. The wind was blowing in gusts but we could talk normally. It was very dark and cold. The rain came down steadily, like water pouring from an inexhaustible bucket.

"I don't know," Carl said. "Have you ever had to take this sort of news before?"

"No."

"I have. There isn't an easy way. You just have to say it."

We had our backs against one of the trees. Carl, Graham and I that is. Ferdie was between his father's knees, lying against the man's chest. We couldn't light cigarettes because of the rain, but we finished my bottle of rum and started on the one Graham had put inside his shirt. Whatever effect the liquor had, wore off quickly in the cold.

"I wonder if Jojo got to him?" I said.

"Probably," Carl said. "He went in pretty quick. Did you try to go in too?"

"Yes. In a way. Not like Jojo. Graham felt me going and stopped me."

"Of course I stop you, Mistah Fabricus. Two men couldn't have help Mistah Oliver more dan one."

"I know. Thanks."

"Dat's all right, sah. You wasn't t'inking. Somebody did have to t'ink for you."

"How is the boy?" I asked.

"Him is fine, sah. Him cold, but nuttin happen to him. You all right, Ferdie?" He was hugging the child close to give him warmth.

"Yes, Pappa," the boy said; his teeth were clicking. It was a painful sound.

"You'd better give him some more of the rum," Carl said.

"Here, Ferdie," Graham said. "Drink dis. Him gwine get drunk, you see."

"Me drink rum before, Pappa."

"Not when I see you , bwoy. If I ever ketch you, it's burn I burn your tail fe' you."

We all laughed in the dark and the rain. We were so cold that the sudden freezing gusts made no difference. It was too cold to even think of Oliver and Jojo clearly. I remember that I thought the island had been lucky. We had only had one blow. The eye of the storm must have been over the sea. When it came in over the land there were two stretches of high wind with a calm between. It was always the second blow which seemed to hurt people most.

Towards morning the wind dropped. It still blew, but fitfully, and it only came as strong breezes. The rain had almost stopped and there were long clouds across the sky, with stars showing between them. The cold had become so bad that we were all standing up, jogging on our toes and slapping ourselves. Graham gave me the rum.

"Drink easy, sah," he said. "Not much left." Oliver had been carrying the other bottle.

"Listen!" Ferdie said. "Listen!" He gripped my arm tightly between his small icy hands. We stopped talking. There was no sound but that from the swollen river and the breeze in the branches. Then drifting up the hillside, I heard a feeble, bad-tempered shout: "Andrew! A-a-andr-e-e-w!" It was Jojo's voice. I yelled back. We went down the hillside. It was still very dark but the torches showed up the ground. The grass looked wild and stamped on. When we came to the gully we had to go very carefully. It was a wide, loudly shouting rapids, and the earth was cut away into it where the dug-out had been.

"A-a-n-dr-e-e-w!"

"Coming!"

We followed the new gully down, casting the torch-beams on the water and the banks as we went. Near the bottom of the slope we found them. A huge cedar had fallen across the water. It must have fallen early in the storm and Jojo and Oliver had been lodged in the enormous spread of its branches as they were swept down to the river. They were half in the water still; Jojo had one arm around Oliver and the other hooked round a branch. He ducked his face as I shone the torch on him.

"For Christ's sake," he said, "stop pissing around and get us out of here."

We crawled along the trunk of the great cedar, Ferdie holding the torches on the gully bank. We climbed in among the branches and hauled them out. It was very difficult because they were both half-paralysed and Oliver was almost unconscious. When we got him to the safe ground and began slapping him, he half-opened his eyes and clucked drowsily, like a hen when you wake her in the middle of the night.

We reached Brandt's Pen late the next afternoon. We were still mounted because the mules had found us before daybreak. They had come down the hillside and began to eat right away. They had found us, but we had lost the dogs and the guns. It took us a long time to reach the Pen because we hadn't been able to ford the river without going far back into the mountains where it was narrow. The countryside looked like a badly used toothbrush. It was fresh and cool, with grey, fat clouds and a warm sun.

We had a lot of food left in the saddle bags and we ate heavily as we rode. The trails were choked with small fallen trees and grass plaited by the wind. In some places the land had slid down from the mountain-sides and we had to dismount and lead the mules. It was very slow travelling.

Nearer the Pen there was less damage; and when we came over Brandt's Peak it only looked as if there had been a heavy, tossing storm that had not troubled the trees much. The river was in flood, though, and the dam, when we got to it, had been torn open and the canal broken. Here there was flood water that came up to the mules' bellies. It was draining off down the hillside but there was still a small lake across the path.

.   .   .   .   .

When we came out above the pasture and the house lay below us, we could see that it had suffered little harm. One of the out-houses had lost its shingles, and a big guango tree in the north pasture was stripped of its branches. But the house was all right, and the green had already begun to come back into the grass. The others were riding across the pasture, and what seemed like the whole of Brandt's Pen was running up to meet them. Sybil and Margaret were keeping with Sheila because she couldn't go very fast. Neither of them looked as if that was where they wanted to be.

The Pen had never been badly hit in a hurricane because it lay under the big peaks, with the mountain wall close behind. The wind always did more damage further down and on the coast.

from THE FACES OF LOVE

Nature

H. D. Carberry

We have neither Summer nor Winter
Neither Autumn nor Spring.
We have instead the days
When the gold sun shines on the lush green canefields —
Magnificently.
The days when the rain beats like bullets on the roofs
And there is no sound but the swish of water in the
    gullies
And trees struggling in the high Jamaica winds.
Also there are the days when leaves fade from off
    guango trees
And the reaped canefields lie bare and fallow to the sun.
But best of all there are the days when the mango and
    the log-wood blossom
When the bushes are full of the sound of bees and the
    scent of honey,
When the tall grass sways and shivers to the slightest
    breath of air,
When the buttercups have paved the earth with yellow
    stars
And beauty comes suddenly and the rains have gone.

Linda's Bedtime

Andrew Salkey

Night fell like an over-ripe mango. It splashed across the hillside and left angular streaks of sunset wedged between the western boundary and the cactus fence. Linda disliked being hustled away to bed at this time. She always played "jump the shadow" when the back yard became lined with uncertain traces of nightfall. Her mother could never understand this.

"Look here, Linda! You are a five-year-old gal pickney, now. No little baby, no more. What wrong with you? Is malice you malice your bed? Why you always kicking up so much fuss when I ready to wash you up?"

"But, Ma, you come and spoil up me game. Every time you come and mash up things. Just when the shadows them so good to pass over, you have to come with bed and wash up. Look how the shadows them nice and bright — just ready to jump over and ride like Cousin Sassy jack."

"You leave shadow and back yard alone. Hear me? When you wake up, them going be there nice as a ninepence, tomorrow. Gal pickney like you have to have a whole heap of sleep 'cause when you grow up and turn woman, you will have all sort of other bad-bad shadow to jump over. Is that time you going need strength to jump and no broke your neck!"

Before Linda would go peacefully to her cot, her mother had to tell her an Anancy story. After the story, her father came in and said the usual "good night prayers". Linda liked praying with her father. She would begin rather seriously, and after the third verse the prayer became a sort of relay for two voices. She would quicken the pace, race ahead of her father, stop suddenly, wait for him to catch up, and then quicken the pace, again.

"You know something, Linda?"

"What, Papa?"

"I can't say that I fancy the way you speeding up the prayers, at all."

"Is nothing really, Papa. I do it like that every night."

"That is just the matter. You have no feelings for good night prayers, at all. Always racing going on like you are a sailor parrot with mouth troubles."

"But, Papa, you say good night prayers like it is a sort of burial going on. Don't you think that it would be better if you say it the way Mama say her Anancy story?"

"I don't understand you, Linda, love."

"Well, Papa, I think that you could say it nice and pretty up with lots of eye movements and heavy breathing and different kinds of voice."

"You know, Linda, I despairing plenty-plenty of your treatment of the word of the Lord. Everything you think of have to have some connexion with that fool-fool spider, Anancy. I want you to understand that Anancy and the Lord who is God son is two different people, entirely. The Lord is no Anancy story. I want you to understand the serious thing that the Lord is."

Linda lowered her eyes and made an inverted V with her hands. She drew a little nearer to her father and whispered: "Papa, I know the difference between Anancy and the Lord, long time ago. Honest! I know it, long time now."

He said: "Linda, love, if that is so, why you doing this thing to me? Why you causing me worry-head and all the botheration?"

"Because I know that you would vex up and wrinkle your eye. I like to watch you when you getting in a temper, Papa. You make up your face like John Connu dancer and you bottom lip hang down and tremble plenty-plenty."

"So you father is a John Connu dancer, now, eh?"

He hugged her tightly and both of them laughed heartily. The laughter attracted Linda's mother who was busy putting away her washing in a large mahogany wash-stand. She banged the sides of the wash-stand and shouted: "What's going on in there! When since good night prayers include belly laugh and sweet joke?"

She came to the doorway and stood with her arms akimbo. Linda winked sheepishly, kissed her father and slipped into her cot. She said: "Mama, you not vex with me? I hope you not vex, because if you really vex I going to ask back for the prayers I say for you, all of them."

"I can see you and your father asking back for the mis-shapen prayers the both of you say, here, tonight. I can just see it. All you would get back is the belly laughing and the sweet joke that you both was offering up."

She knelt beside the cot and kissed Linda. She fussed with the sheets and patted the pillow. She took her husband by his left hand and led him towards the veranda.

from **A QUALITY OF VIOLENCE**

Acceptance

Neville Dawes

I praise the glorious summers of pimento
Sun-purple, riper than the wet red clay-smell
Of my youth by cornlight and river-run
As dog and I, we screamed the small green hill
And the salt smooth wind from the leaping sea
Sang in the yellow sunflower.

I praise the dumb scared child made me
In coffee-groves, and the barbecues of graves,
Smelling of ghosts' old country flesh, laid
By my father for his tribe (fictitious as angels);
A small all-alone boy riding to harvest hymns
In the green of the day as the shackle-bell tongued
On the churchy hill-top.

I praise the legends we made
When the drunk hawks and worse were merry
Waltzed up the day
Halloed the mountains of birds and the nestling curve
    of the reeling river
Swam, those eyes reading the first garden's blush and
    Adam's.
When weathers twisted the old thunder-voice
I was King Arthur's irrelevant steed on the lightning
    page
Castling
All races, all men, the drunk hawks and worse
Climbing together the top of the colourless rain
To the dappling sun.

I praise all this
Returning in a shower of mango-blossoms —
The creaking village, the old eyes, the graves, the sun's
    kiss —
And lonely as ever, as the bare cedars,
I walk by the stream (where boys still plash
Dusking and falling in a star-apple sunset),
And find her there, ancient as the lost lands,
Bandannaed and gray and calling:
Then I read the monumental legend of her love
And grasp her wrinkled hands.

Rosalie Gidharee

Michael Anthony

It was about a week afterwards, when, on coming out into the road I saw the *dougla* girl under the cashew tree. I walked towards the cashew tree to go down the hill to the shops. She was stooping and she had her dress fixed carefully to cover her knees and she appeared to be breaking off the nuts from the fallen cashews. As I passed she looked up and I said, "Hello."

"Hello," she said, and she smiled. I slowed down, and she said, "You is the feller who went with Pa?"

"Yes. In Cedar Grove? Yes, that's me."

"He was talking about you all the time," she said. Her smile was very warm and there seemed to be laughter in her eyes.

"I had a nice time in Cedar Grove."

"Everybody does have a nice time with Pa. Pa funny too bad."

I was not going down to the shops for anything in particular. In fact, it was only when I had seen her that I had decided to walk down to the shops. Seeing how simple and easy-going she was, I was encouraged to stay and talk. I pretended to be calm but I was somewhat tense inside.

She had been gathering cashew nuts. Now she continued doing this, and everytime she stooped she carefully pulled down her dress over her knees.

"You not going to this Government School?" she said.

"Not yet."

"Pa said you from Down-the-beach."

"Aha."

"Radix?"

"Yes."

"So you going to the RC."

"Aha."

She had several nuts now in a heap on the ground, and now she stood up again and she was trying to wipe out the cashew stains from her hand. I was feeling awkward, with nothing to say, and I was just wondering whether I should go, when I saw someone like Lennard coming up the hill.

"Lennard coming," I said.

She dashed to a tree and picked a leaf. She seemed suddenly full of play. She looked all around her and then she saw him coming, and she stood looking towards him, gigglingly, with both hands behind her back.

As Lennard drew near I saw that he had a whip in one hand and a leaf in the other. He, too, had the giggles. She said to me, "We cut *green-leaf*."

"Yes, I know."

From the time she had dashed to get the leaf I had known what was going on, for we had this game at our school. Her face was bright with playfulness. For a moment I hated everything.

As Lennard came up he scrutinized her with his eyes. They were both grinning and she was holding up her green leaf in front of her, and as he had his own, neither of them bothered to say, "Green-leaf!" Lennard raised his whip, jokingly, as if to hit her, and she jumped away and he tried to get hold of her but she slipped from him and ran a little way up the road. Then she broke off a hibiscus limb to threaten him with. As she came back again Lennard said to me, "I didn't know you know Rosa."

"'Rosa' for my friends," she said, 'Rosalie" to you — if you please.'

"She is a nice little jane," Lennard said to me. "Going to the school fair, Ro?"

"Look if you call me a nice jane again I'll go and tell Pa!"

"Don't bother about old man Gidharee," he told me.

"But look at this boy!" Rosalie cried. "Don't be fresh!"

"Set those dogs on him," I joked.

"She wouldn't do that. Serious now, Rosa, you going to the fair Discovery Day?"

"All depends," she said. "You?"

"But sure," Lennard said.

Rosalie turned to me: "You?"

"Ah — yes," I said. I did not even know about the fair.

Lennard had hardly taken his eyes off her since he had arrived. Now he said, "All depends on what, Ro?"

"On if I feel like."

"Well you better feel like!"

"Why? To please who?" She put her arms akimbo and tilted up her chin at him.

"To please *me*," Lennard said.

"Ah, drop dead!"

Lennard made a grab for her and she scampered up the road. Then he left her alone.

She came back and she bent to pick up her heap of cashew nuts. She bent down most carefully and delicately. She was going to put the nuts in her dress, holding the front of her dress like a bowl, when, probably remembering us, she changed her mind. For she would have had to hold up the front of her dress a little, and she certainly would not want to do that with us there. She tried to scoop up the nuts with both hands, and finally getting all in, she stood up.

"See you, gentlemen," she said.

"You calling *me*, gentleman?" Lennard said. "Don't depend on that."

"I'm not talking to *you*."

"He is not any gentleman neither," Lennard said. "Boy, you is any gentleman?"

I just laughed.

Rosalie said: "You is always some spokesman for somebody. Let him talk for himself. Anyway I must go. See you fellers."

She skipped across the road.

Lennard said, "Rosa."

She stood up.

"Stay a little bit," he said.

"For what?"

I could see Lennard wanted me to go away now. Rosalie stood looking at him with raised eyebrows, and he said nothing and I guessed it was because I was there. So I said, "Look, I'll see you fellers some time," and moved off.

I ambled down towards the shops.

.   .   .   .

It seemed like many days afterwards, when, on going out after the cashew, I saw Rosalie Gidharee in the road. She must have only just walked out of her gateway, for after a moment the brown dog, Lion, came springing out after her, frisking about and playing with her. She cried: "Lion, stop! *Stop*! Stop it, Lion!" But the dog kept on frisking and growling and playing with her. She picked up a piece of twig from the roadside and Lion ran away.

"He only *playing* with you," I said, from near the cashew tree. She did not quite hear me. I said it from there mainly to draw her away from her gateway, and towards where I was. She put her hands to her ears to show she did not hear.

"Come up here," I said boldly.

She still did not hear but she began walking towards the cashew tree.

I had had a stone in my hand ready to pelt the cashew with, but I dropped this now and began thinking what to say to her. She was wearing a blue skirt and sailor bodice and she looked wonderful and new and strange. It was a brilliant morning, and behind her the drop of the hill was gradual, then severe, and the sun was just climbing the edge of the far trees.

She was near up now and she said, "Sorry. Couldn't hear you. What's that you was saying?"

"The dog," I said. "Lion was only playing with you."

"Oh, Lion. Lion too blinking frisky."

I laughed. As she stood there she seemed so simple and pure. I supposed that as she said "blinking" she thought she had said quite a lot. Her skirt was longish and I guessed it was her sister's. There was a big girl in their house and I reasoned this must be her sister. Rosalie had pulled in the skirt at the waist, to take up the slack, and had pinned it up. I was a bit surprised because she was not at all self-conscious, and yet other girls were always fussing about how they looked. I was glad to see her like this, with the long skirt, and the safety-pin showing. The bodice fitted neatly over her slightly-rising chest, and as I glanced over her, she seemed perfect in every way.

Her eyes were not on me now, but on the ground. She was looking for cashew nuts. She walked around, pouncing whenever she saw a cashew, and my eyes followed her. Then abruptly she said: "Why you don't pelt your cashew."

"Why?"

"Don't bother about me. Pelt your cashew."

I was embarrassed. I said nothing. I just stood looking at her, pretending to be puzzled.

She said: "Or if you want me to go — "

"You don't have to go, Rosalie."

She turned looking at me in the same way she had looked at Lennard that time when he had asked her to stay. She knew she was pretty. She knew we were all frantic over her. I cursed myself for letting her see how silly I was.

After a while I said, "Where's Lennard? I ain't seen him for days."

"Somewhere around, perhaps."

"He ain't come up to see you?" I felt my voice tremble.

"To see me? Why?"

And then with sudden rashness, I said, "Well, you is his jane."

To my surprise she still stood there. She did not storm away. She looked at me calmly and said, "*His* jane? Lennard only fresh!"

I was suddenly relieved that she was not angry, and then even more relieved by what she had said. Now she looked up in my face and slanted her head, and her arms were akimbo. "He told you that?"

"No. Oh no. I just said that."

"What make you say that."

"Just pulling your legs."

"He *said* it. O God, boy, just tell me if he really said that!"

"No, not really. I was only making a little joke with you."

"Well that's a funny kinda joke to make," she said.

Presently, she seemed to forget all about it, and she began looking up at the ripe cashews on the tree.

"Oo," she said, "look at that nice one up there."

"I'll pick it for you."

"Not for me. I don't like cashew. Not these. These too *rack*."

"I'll pick it for you for the nut."

"Oh, not so much trouble for that little nut!"

"I'll pelt it down anyway."

I started pelting again. As I pelted I was thinking of lots of things and I was not really caring for the cashew. I was thinking about Joe and Rosalie and I wondered if I should ask her about Joe. I thought I'd better not. I thought of Lennard and how she had reacted about him, and then other things came to mind. Then all of a sudden that big poster on the shop down the hill came to mind and it was about the Discovery Day fair. It was stuck against the shop and it said in fancy lettering: GRAND DISCOVERIE FAYRE AND DANCE. This had stirred me mainly because of the quaintness of the writing and because Rosalie and Lennard had talked about the fair. I turned round to Rosalie and found her looking at me.

"So Monday's the fair?"

"Oh gosh, yes. Yes. You going?"

"Don't know, really. You?"

"Yes. Come on, boy — why not?"

"I mightn't be able to come."

"Why?"

"Pa might be going to hospital," I said, and a wave of sadness swept upon me.

"What happen?"

"Pa sick. Bad."

"I know. My Pa was saying something about that. Sorry."

I said nothing, but looked the other way towards the hill. This was one of those horrible moments of grief that now and again broke over me. My father's suffering hurt me greatly. No doctor seemed able to cure him. Instead of getting better he worsened every day.

"He'll be all right," Rosalie said. "For all you know he'll be soon all right. You know what I mean. I mean I know how you feeling."

I was still looking towards the hills. I bit my lips and there was a little burning in my nose.

"Don't worry," she said, "he'll get better."

I stood silent.

As old as I was, often when I thought of Pa's illness, I lost all calmness. Now I was holding the tears at bay, and the phase was passing. I heard a deep bark and I looked round and it was Rover who had come out into the road. Seeing Rosalie he scampered towards her. Before he reached her she cried: "Rover! Look here, *Rover!*" Rover stopped short and he seemed to understand that she did not want to play. He looked up at her, wagging his tail. I was feeling better now. "Rove," I said. He wagged his tail more violently but he did not come. He was wanting to frolic with Rosalie. But she was not in the mood.

"Rover feeling frisky," I said.

"I'll give him 'frisky'," she said.

Rover stood up in front of her, looking up at her. She said sternly: "You better go back inside, eh!"

He still stood there, wagging his tail and his whole bottom.

I said, "So you old man stayed home today, Rosalie?"

"Yes."

I had reasoned that out because of the dogs. Mr Gidharee never went to Cedar Grove without those dogs. Having seen Lion and Rover I knew he was at home. I was sure that Tiger, the lazy one, was sunning himself somewhere.

"You all doesn't keep those dogs tied?"

"Sometimes. Not always."

"You never know, you know. If anybody just wander in your yard, they could be dangerous."

"That's why we have them," she said, "that's just why."

I laughed. I said, "Four good Tobago dogs — major!"

"'*Good*' Tobago dogs? You mean 'good-for-nothing'!"

"That is four *good* dogs," I said, seriously, "four champion dogs. Anybody could see that."

"Maybe," she said casually. "*We* like them, anyway."

She did not have the cashew nuts in her hands now and I did not know what she had done with them. She had gathered a few when she had first come. I only thought of this now as she moved off to go. Although my mind was not quite free of my father, I felt a certain pain on account of her, too.

She said, "Think I'm going in — else Dolly will start screaming for me like mad."

"Oh, that girl is your sister?"

"Yes — you like her?"

"Not her, somebody else."

She pretended she did not hear. "Think I'm going in, boy."

"All right, Rosalie Gidharee."

"And what's your other name — I don't mean 'Shellie', I mean, Shellie what?"

"Shellie anything you like."

"Okay Mr Anything-you-like," she said; and she went in.

from GREEN DAYS BY THE RIVER

The Pawpaw

Edward Kamau Brathwaite

Four little boys, tattered,
Fingers and faces splattered
With mud, had climbed
In the rain and caught
A pawpaw which they brought,
Like a bomb, to my house. I saw
Them coming: a serious, mumbling,
Tumbling bunch who stopped
At the steps in a hunch.
Releasing the fruit from the leaf
It was wrapped in, I watched them
Carefully wash the pawpaw
Like a nugget of gold. This done,
With rainwater, till it shone
They climbed on into the house
To present the present to me.
A mocking sign of the doom of all flesh?
Or the purest gold in the kingdom?

World's End

Roger Mais

It was a cheerless morning, the sky was overcast with grey opaque vapour like a veil. Every third person or so that you passed in the street coughed, and each one seemed as dispirited as the next. You saw the sadness of people now, even under the casual laughter and the bravado of indifference.

Old Ben walked along without looking to the right or left of him, and the boy pattered along behind. He had forgotten that he had not had any breakfast, and that he was hungry. He walked with the sort of aimless desperation of a man who has nowhere to go; but it seemed to him necessary, although barren of result.

The boy, uncomplaining, walked always a little behind; reminded old Ben of his presence by suddenly giving way to a fit of coughing, precipitated by that tickling burning feeling in his throat. Ben stopped, suddenly remembered the boy and breakfast; remembered that Tim must be hungry; thinking suddenly of hunger, emptiness, his own loss, and his emptiness in a world of emptiness, passing from one bleak façade to the next, a shop.

They went inside, and Ben bought a threepenny loaf of bread, paid threepence more and the Chinaman obligingly cut the loaf right in two down the middle length-wise and smeared butter on both sides facing, clamped them together shut, and Ben taking, broke the loaf in two, passed one portion to the boy.

They ate breaking pieces out of the loaf with finger and thumb, chewing solidly with steady unbroken rhythm of facial muscles, like men who are at the business of eating, the utterly simplified motions of necessity, eating; without waste of energy, without loss of motion, getting the business done.

They left the shop, walking the streets again, eating their breakfast as they went.

Sudden lighting sun breaking now, putting their shadows behind them. Coming out of the mist of vapour-like veil, welcome, another and necessary. No loss here, either, no waste of motion. They quickened their pace, as though an urgency compelled, another necessity thrust upon them, to suit their pace to the sun.

The next place of call going the round of his regular customers, the yard in which three separate families lived. He knocked on the gate. A young woman came out, not recognizing him; a man too, walking towards him coming from the back of the premises.

"Why, it is Mass Ben! How-do, Mass Ben. Where you' cart is," said the woman.

"Ah, me daughter."

"I didn't know it was who. What happen?"

"Nothing today? What become of you' cart?" said the man.

Both of them saying the same things, asking the same questions; always the same. They had not recognized him, either. He passed it on with the barest lift of his shoulders.

"Donkey died las' night. Got bellyache. Jus' lay down an' died."

"You mean it!" The man made a sound with his tongue against his teeth. The woman said nothing, to her scarcely something of matter, the death of a donkey. So it had been the same everywhere he went, calling at each house on a barren and useless mission, but to him necessary.

At each house he had stopped he had recited the same thing. His donkey had died in the night. No more cart, no more yams, potatoes, cabbages, cho-cho for sale, or anything; no more business, nothing to do. Nothing to live by from day to day, buying and selling his goods. And he thought it unquestionable and necessary that they should know. And the same questions asked always, and the same answers.

"What you going to do now?"

He hadn't had time to think about that. It was odd that they should all think of the same things to say; or was it? He hadn't had time to give that matter a thought. They spoke about it sympathetically, jokingly, like the man and the woman here.

"You could sell the skin. They give you ten shillings for it at the tannery, I hear say," said the man.

"Ten shillings," said Ben, saying the words over in his mouth, but without meaning. What did ten shillings have to do with the matter, where was the connection? He was talking about something else, surely.

"Ten shillings is not to be sneezed at," said the man. Of course not, was anybody saying it wasn't so! But there was always this fact, and that was another, and there was no slightest connection between the two.

He looked stupid, standing there, blinking at them in the sun. The boy stood a little apart, looking on, as though he wasn't involved.

"When is the funeral?" said the woman, and laughed. Looking at his stupid old face she couldn't help laughing. He was funny.

"Funeral?" said old Ben.

And when he said that you couldn't help feeling what a stupid old man he was. The woman laughed again, and went inside.

They left that house and went on to the next, and the rest of them in this street, and then they left this street and went on to the next, and so on, walking useless miles.

About noon the sun came out bright. The day cleared. The boy came abreast of him catching his attention by tugging at his sleeve.

"Papa, let us go home now," he said.

"You tired, boy?"

"No. But let us go home all the same."

"But how can we. We still have places to go; wait; I know what. You must be hungry again, we will stop and eat."

"I am not hungry," the boy said.

But he couldn't explain anything more to the old man. When the people laughed he felt a curious sense of shame, although he always stood aloof from it as though he were not involved. He too looking at that helpless, stupid old face blinking in the sun, felt it; but he didn't laugh. It came as a raw revelation; he had never thought of his papa in this way before — seeing him so now, he was ashamed for his father and for himself. He was conscious always of the others' laughter, and his own shame.

He tried again to persuade the old man.

"Let us go home now, Papa," he begged, but old Ben either would not or could not bring his mind to this, there was always only that other.

"We will get another donkey," the boy wheedled as an older person might try to coax a petulant child. "We will get us another donkey, Papa," tugging at his sleeve to bring his attention back to him.

They went into a shop and the old man bought a threepenny loaf of bread and a small parcel of brown sugar. He borrowed a quart measure from the buxom woman who served in the shop, and drew water from a tap in the yard. He put the sugar in the water and stirred it, and with this beverage they washed down the bread.

After they had eaten they sat on the shop piazza and rested. The old man leaned back against the wall and closed his eyes. The boy sat upright, alert, watching the old man.

A fly settled on his nose, and he came awake suddenly. He rubbed the back of his hand against his nose and sat up. It was raining now, he saw. He hadn't known when it had started to rain, so he must have been asleep. The boy was sitting across from him, his face was screwed up, crying.

"What this," said the old man. "What you crying for?"

"Nothing," said the boy.

"You cry for nothing, then," said the old man. "What sense to cry for nothing, boy?"

The boy sniffed loudly, without shame. Some people sheltering on the shop piazza from the rain looked down incuriously at the old man and the boy.

The old man said in a gruff voice: "Here, son, you want a penny?" He said, "I wouldn't have brought you out at all, if I knew you was goin' to cry."

The boy sat dejectedly rubbing his eyes.

"Here, you want a penny?"

"No," said the boy.

"What you want, then?"

"I want to go home."

"Well, bless me," the old man said. "I thought you was crying for something."

Then he started to upbraid the boy, calling him names, saying he was no son of his, to make a spectacle of himself like that before people.

"They are laughing at you," said the old man. "Shut it up this minute, you hear, before I clout you on the head."

Presently the boy stopped crying.

"Here's a penny," the old man said.

The boy took the coin and put it in his pocket.

"Well, bless me," said the old man.

The boy coughed; and the old man grumbled under his breath about people catching their death of cold walking in the rain.

"Can't go home until it stops raining," said the old man querulously.

As though it was a cue for which he was unconsciously waiting, the boy started coughing again. He coughed and coughed.

The rain beat down on the zinc roof in a steady downpour that drowned out every other sound.

"See what you would have caught? Must be want your death of cold," the old man grumbled.

The sun came out and it stopped raining. And the people who

were sheltering on the shop piazza moved along — all except the old man and the boy. People came and went, a trickle of people passing all the time, but still the old man and the boy sat on.

Presently the old man went inside the shop. The boy remained outside with a curious aloofness, his hands thrust in his pockets, looking out into the street.

As twilight closed in the street seemed to shrink, to become narrower, as though the sidewalks had drawn closer.

Inside the shop the old man was explaining to the woman behind the counter about the loss of his donkey, the loss of his business, and the fact that there was no money, and the woman listened without laughing. Nor did she try to tell him that the skin would fetch him ten shillings at the tannery. She just listened while the old man talked and talked, with awareness in his intelligent eyes.

Outside on the piazza the boy stood listlessly watching the dusk closing in on the street, and the people coming and going, and sometimes stopping to greet each other passing the good of the day, conversing. A dray drove furiously down the street and people gave way on either side, so that the yelling drayman flourishing and cracking his whip seemed like a charioteer driving through the opposing ranks of an enemy horde.

The stars came out one by one and filled the sky.

Inside the shop the old man babbled on, reciting the inexhaustible tale of his loss — like a man relating the story of it, who had witnessed the end of the world.

Ten years ago, he said, he had buried his wife. She had been a good woman, and they had had three sons. They had buried one while he was still at the breast; the last. Seven years after his eldest son, the apple of his eye, had died, leaving only the boy, that was Tim. Tim was all he had left. There was now only himself and Tim. All his life he seemed to have accumulated nothing but losses, there was no money, nothing to show for it all. Last evening he had stabled the donkey, he said, and before dark it had laid down with the bellyache, and died. It was a good donkey, he said, gentle and amiable as a lamb. He had had it seven years.

There Runs a Dream

A. J. Seymour

There runs a dream of perished Dutch plantations
In these Guiana rivers to the sea.
Black waters, rustling through the vegetation
That towers and tangles banks, run silently
Over lost stellings where the craft once rode
Easy before trim dwellings in the sun
And fields of indigo would float out broad
To lose the eye right on the horizon.

These rivers know that strong and quiet men
Drove back a jungle, gave Guiana root
Against the shock of circumstance, and then
History moved down river, leaving free
The forest to creep back, foot by quiet foot
And overhang black waters to the sea.

George and the Bicycle Pump

Earl Lovelace

When he left work, George walked across the road from the
printery, paid for an *Evening News* with a dollar bill, and with just
a glance at its headlines, began to fold the paper to put it in his
pocket, while Mary, the vendor, whom he had awakened from a
snatched moment of slumber, fumbled almost distractedly among
the tins and bottles on her tray for the eighty cents change to give
him. He watched her gather with merciless patience, one by one,
a set of coins from a small biscuit tin next to her stock of
cigarettes, then unearth a twenty–five cents piece from below a
jar of dinnermints. She was just reaching into her bosom to
continue her search when in a fit of mercy, George said, "Give
me dinnermints for the balance of the change."

"You want dinnermints for the change?" she asked, her voice
fumbly, appealing, tired, as if the thought, each thought was a
weight to be contemplated before it was lifted; so that George,
feeling his own shoulders sag under the burden of her effort,
pointed to a bowl of Tobago plums in front of her, "Look," he
said. "Gimme some of those plums instead." But, his earlier
request had penetrated. With one hand poised suddenly above
the jar with the dinnermints, she showed him a face appealing for
mercy and with the promise of tears. "All right," he said, quickly,
as if wanting to pull back his last request. "Give me the
dinnermints." And he watched her count again with timeless
exactitude the ten cents and twenty–five cents and five cents
pieces, while his hand remained stretched out to receive them;
and she didn't look up until she had extracted, from the store of
her inexhaustible patience, the number of dinnermints that
equalled the value of the money he was owed; and now, she
would count them out again, the coins first, then the sweets, as
she pressed them one by one into his open palm. So that he
found himself wondering if he would ever get away to the
Savannah to see his team play their football game.

At last it was over. George dropped the dinnermints and

change into the same pocket, crossed the street and, hurrying now, went into the lot at the side of the printery, where he had his bicycle parked. As soon as his eyes fell on the bicycle, he saw that, yes, the pump was missing; and it came to him now, with the calm sadness as at a death, that, yes, its absence now was to be explained only by theft. "They thief my bicycle pump," he whispered.

Seven weeks ago, when the first pump disappeared from his bicycle, George was certain that one of the fellars from the printery had borrowed it and forgotten to put it back. He was furious, Suppose he had a flat?

"Suppose I had a flat?" he asked at the printery next morning. You borrow a pump; you mean is such a hard thing to put it back?" And for most of the day he went about the printery with an air of righteousness and injury, lecturing everybody on responsibility and consideration, and it never occurred to him that the disappearance of his bicycle pump might be explained in any way other than the one he had theorised until Marcos, the supervisor and a friend for the fifteen years he was at the printery and for the two years before, when as young fellars they both started out at *The Chronicle*, pulled him aside and said to him, "George, nobody here ain't borrow your bicycle pump."

"Somebody had to borrow it," he said to Beulah when he got home that evening. "The pump just can't walk away."

"They thief your bicycle pump, George." Beulah looked up from her sewing, her eyes gleaming with the personal triumph she exuded whenever she suspected that he was in the wrong. "They thief it!" with a sense of victory, as if it was something she had predicted.

"Thief? Thief my pump? You see you . . . *your* mind. Thief is the first thing that come to *your* mind."

Beulah was sewing a dress for her niece who was getting married in Mamoral in two weeks. She held up the garment to bite off a loose end of the thread. "Where you had it?" she asked, the thread still gripped between her teeth. "Where you had the pump, George?" She had a talent for making his simplest action appear to be the most criminal stupidity.

"I had it . . . ." George felt like a child. He didn't even want to answer her, "I had it on the bicycle."

"You leave your bicycle pump on your bicycle?" She had put down the dress and was looking at him. "I don't believe you, George." And with a sigh she bent her head to her sewing, pressed a foot to the pedal of her foot machine, sending the noise whirring throughout the house. Not another word. She had ended the communication.

But, that was Beulah. To her the world outside of Mamoral, where she was born, was a jungle from which her only refuge was the fortress of her house. Here in the city, she kept her windows closed, curtains drawn, doors locked; and whatever business she had with the world outside was transacted through a parted curtain over the open louvres next to her front door. How she didn't suffocate inside the house, he didn't know. As soon as he got home from work, his first task was to open the windows. As soon as he turned his back, she closed them.

To Beulah, the theft of George's bicycle pump (for she had no doubt that it was theft) was a signal that the criminals of the world were closing in on them, that somehow they had become people marked for further distress, and in that week whenever George went out on the porch to the rocking chair, she locked the front door. He had to knock to get back into the house.

George still held to the theory that someone had borrowed his pump, and that the culprit, not wanting to own up to the responsibility, had found it simpler to keep quiet. As he told Marcos, "Not everybody have the courage to accept their wrong. A person do one wrong, a little, small inch of a wrong and they frighten to correct it, and that is what start them on the road to crime. But, believe me, Marcos, I wouldn't ask no question. I wouldn't vex, it will just be great if whoever borrow the pump, just bring it back and put it on the cycle. It will be real great."

"George," Marcos interrupted, for George was going on and on. "I tell you already, nobody here ain't borrow your bicycle pump."

George, however, believed otherwise and he expected that any evening he would find the pump back in its place on the bicycle. After two weeks and no sign of the pump, George bought a new pump and fitted it on the bicycle. If he missed this one also, then he would know for sure that the first one was really stolen.

"I see you still leaving the pump on your bicycle," Beulah said. "You shame to walk with it in your hand? You shame to put it in your pocket?"

At the wedding of her niece the previous weekend, with relatives all around and everybody making nearly as much fuss over her as over the bride, she had put on a performance that convinced everybody that she and George were two love birds, and even after they returned to Port of Spain, she had continued to be civil to him. It was that peace that George found himself now straining to keep.

"Is fifteen years I parking my bicycle in the printery. I never walk with no pump. I lock the bicycle, yes, but I never walk with the pump." He heard himself and was ashamed. He was whining.

"You knows best," she said. "Leave it there for them to thief. You rich. You could afford a new pump every week."

George made for the porch. There on the old rocking chair, he watched the evening grow still and fussy and felt the heat come up and watched the sun set. He sat in the darkness, not bothering to turn on the lights, waiting to feel so sleepy that when he went into the furnace of a house, it would be to go directly to bed. He couldn't enter. Beulah had locked the front door. He began to bang on the door. He was real angry. "But, I right here. I right here, what you have to lock the door for?"

"George, you don't think I see you sleeping there on yourself in that rocking chair. You ain't read where they tie up a woman inside her own house and thief all her jewelry. Her husband sleeping on the gallery, and the thief just waltz past him and tie her up and take her jewelry and leave him sleeping there. You didn't read it?"

"Well, is best I go and live in the jail."

"I don't know about you," said Beulah. "But I prefer jail to the cemetry."

George was really angry. He went back out on the porch. "And leave the blasted door," he said.

"Listen, man," said Beulah, who could always give better than she got," is not I who thief your bicycle pump. Don't take your vexation out on me."

"Thief?" George tried to laugh. "Who say anybody thief the pump?"

The next evening he went to get his bicycle, he found that the new pump, the one he had bought just a couple days before, was gone. For a moment, he stood in shock; then, the impulse came over him to steal somebody else's pump, anyone's. There were five bicycles parked in the lot. He went to the first one. There was no pump on it. He turned to the next. Not one of the bicycles had a pump. He felt his body grow chill and a bottomless space open up inside him and he was falling through it.

120

"I don't have a word to say," Beulah said when she saw the pump was missing. "Not a word."

Out on the rocking chair, George began to wonder about the pumps. Who had removed them? Was it a thief? If it was, on what days did he make his rounds? Was he someone who set out to steal or did he just happen upon the pumps? Who was it that had removed the first pump? Was it the same person who had taken the second one? Was the first pump borrowed and the second one stolen? Or were both borrowed, or both stolen? I wonder, he thought, with a bit of pride, if he doesn't wonder what kind of fellar it is who leaving his pump on his bicycle? I wonder if he knows that that fellar is me?

"And by the way, George." Beulah was standing in the doorway, "I take out some money from the bank today. We have to put in burglar–proofing."

"Tomorrow," said George, "I buying another pump."

So he had bought another pump. This time, though, he set out to catch the thief, if thief it was. At odd moments he would jump up from his linotype machine and rush outside to the parking lot and his bicycle. At other times with an air of nonchalance, he would steal forth softly. He organised a variety of weapons to be at hand whenever he went into the parking lot. At one point he had hidden a stick, at another, an old hammer with a long piece of pipe iron as a handle. He put stones at definite points. He made a slingshot which he kept in the drawer of his desk. He drew diagrams detailing points from which he might approach the bicycle. He used his lunch hour to patrol the street in front of the printery. He studied the passersby. He noted all strangers who came into the printery. He questioned them. How suspicious everyone looked. Look at them, he thought, as he watched people go by in front of the printery, one of them is the one who thief my bicycle pump.

For four weeks George kept up his surveillance. The slightest sound from outside would send him in a panic to investigate his bicycle. Fellars, noticing this pattern, began to bang things just to watch him jump. Workers started to become suspicious of him. Some thought that he was slacking, others, with more imagination, decided that he was smuggling something out of the printery, though, what it was, they couldn't tell. Even Marcos became concerned.

"George," Marcos said to him, "your wife giving you trouble or what? Why you don't take a few days' sick leave and rest yourself."

At the end of the day he was exhausted. Home was no release, and he would sit on the rocking chair and watch the burglar–proofing creeping around the house, making it, each day, into more of a prison. He had just begun to relax in the last few days; now, the bicycle pump was gone.

George unlocked the bicycle. He thought that he would be angry. Instead, there was a strange release, a kind of freedom, a peace. Then, rage surged in him, at the world, at the city, at Beulah, at the bicycle. And then he felt sorry for the bicycle and for the world and for Beulah and he thought of the thief. He tried to feel sorry for the thief, to feel superior to him; but, he didn't feel that feeling. He looked around at where he had hidden the stick and the hammer, and he saw the little heaps of stones that he had arranged so subtly as to blend into the lot, and it was for himself that he felt sorry.

George pushed his bicycle out of the lot, no longer hurrying to get to the football game, feeling that in his present state, if he went to the game, he would bring bad luck to his team. It was just a second division team, some young fellars from his part of Belmont, that he had been supporting for the last three years, but, so quietly, so shyly that although the crowds at their games were small and everyone seemed to know everyone else, no one knew him. The only time one of the players noticed him, to his surprise, was last season after they had lost a big game, a final, to John-John. He was making his way out of the Savannah when one of the players, going past him, put a hand on his shoulder and said, "Hard game, uncle. Hard game!" and went on.

George walked, pushing the bicycle, all the way to the Savannah. At last he came to an empty bench below an overhanging samaan tree. He leaned his bicycle against the Savannah rails and went to the bench, but the scent of urine drove him back and with a sigh and a sense of adventure, he went a little way off and perched on the rails, took out his *Evening News* and began to read. From the corners of his eyes, he saw a young policeman approaching with easy authorative, rhythmic steps. Their eyes met, and something in their meeting made George feel a sense of guilt, in need of a defence. He turned back to his newspaper and waited for the policeman to go on. The policeman stopped. He looked at the bicycle. He looked at George. George looked up.

"Why you think they put benches there?" asked the policeman.

"Why they put benches . . .?" George didn't know what he was talking about.

"Those rails," said the policeman. "They have benches there for sitting down. That is why these rails always breaking down."

George hopped off the rails. He felt stupid, guilty. He didn't know that he had been committing an offence. Look at that, eh? Harassing me for sitting down on the Savannah rails, and all over the place people thiefing, George thought as he went past a bench with a broken seat to one with the sun shining on it and sat down.

As soon as he began to read his *News*, a fellar came and sat himself down next to him. He was barefooted, with no shirt under his grimy jacket. As soon as he sat down, he put his face in his hands. Younger than me, George thought. Mad, maybe. All of this from one glance, and he went back to his papers.

"Gimme one of your cigarettes!"

The fellar's glaring eyes were fixed upon him.

"What you say?" An edge was in George's voice.

"I say, 'Chief, gimme one of your cigarettes, please.'"

George was going to say no when he realised that the fellar was pointing at the cigarette pack outlined in his breast pocket. George took out the pack, removed one cigarette and gave it to him.

"You have a light?" Not, 'Chief' anymore, George thought.

George had a lighter. He didn't want the fellar to touch it, so he lit the cigarette for him, and watched him drag greedily on the cigarette, then blow out smoke with a great noise. George hated people to smoke like that. There was a young fellar at the printery who smoked in that greedy, noisy way. Just for that, George never gave him a cigarette. George wanted to get up. He saw the fellar studying him. He hesitated. He didn't want his getting up to make the fellar feel offended.

"What is the headline?"

Relaxed, self–satisfied, smoke issuing from his nostrils, the fellar was looking at him. George held up the paper for him to see, but said, all the same, "Thieves escape with three hundred dollars from El Soccoro gas station."

"Three hundred? Think the police will catch them?" his tone suddenly familiar.

"I dunno."

"Most times the police does get tip off and they know just where to look." With a kind of confidentiality, he added, "They pay you for tipping off, you know."

For no reason that he could think of, George said," You know they thief my bicycle pump today?"

The fellar grew alert, "You have a markonit?"

"A what?"

"A mark. You have a mark on it?"

"A mark? On a bicycle pump?"

"If you don't have a mark on it, then, it not yours, because, then, you see you can't identify it. When you go and make a report to the police, you have to know what it is you loss, and how you will know if you don't have a mark on it. Whenever you buy a bicycle pump, always put a mark on it."

To this piece of wisdom, George nodded.

"Everything I buy I have a mark on it."

George nodded again. Faintly, from behind him, he could hear the roar of a crowd, "Somebody score," he said. He was wondering how his team was doing.

"Chief, you have a little change?" The fellar had on his face a confident, expectant look, as if he was asking for fees owed him for his legal advice.

George sized him up, feeling a kind of power, a kind of shame.

"Like they score another goal again," the fellar said, smiling, his broken teeth coming into prominence, making him look guilty and smug.

But George was looking at two fellars passing. One had a

bicycle pump tucked in at his waist, between his belt.

"Chief, the change," the fellar said.

George stood up and put a hand into his pocket and came upon the dinnermints he had bought from Mary. To give the dinnermints would, he felt, suggest too great a familarity, as if they were friends. He felt for the coins, the change from the dollar bill, and he extracted every penny of it from his pocket and he put it all into the fellar's hand, coin by coin, the way Mary had given it to him. Then he went to his bicycle.

People had started to make their way home from the Savannah. George turned his bicycle towards Belmont. At the traffic lights he joined a number of cyclists and pedestrians waiting for the green. And for a moment he felt himself alive, in the thick of things, with the young fellars talking about the game they had just seen, a boy eyeing a girl, mothers with small children, the roar of passing vehicles, cyclists waiting to sprint across the street. A few brave souls, finding the lights taking too long to change, had begun to walk across the road. The traffic stopped for them and the lights turned green and George crossed in the stream of people. He gave his bicycle a little push, then hopped onto the saddle. He took a dinnermint from his pocket and began to take off the paper in which it was wrapped. Beulah was right, you can't leave your bicycle pump on your bicycle. All those people with pumps in their hands and at their waists, all of them were right. He put the dinnermint in his mouth, crumpled the paper and put it in his pocket.

At home, Beulah unlocked the door for him.

"They thief my bicycle pump," he said.

"You sure they thief it?"

He didn't respond to her irony. He didn't say anything.

"Buy another pump and leave it on your bicycle again," she said, trying to draw him out. "They will thief it again."

"Let them thief it," he said, as he heard the burglar-proofing clang shut behind him, then thinking that it was cheaper to pay for a bicycle pump than to see the end of the world.

As John to Patmos

Derek Walcott

As John to Patmos, among the rocks and the blue live
    air hounded
His heart to peace, as here surrounded
By the strewn silver on waves, the wood's crude hair,
    the rounded
Breasts of the milky bays, palms, flocks, and the green
    and dead

Leaves, the sun's brass coin on my cheek, where
Canoes brace the sun's strength, as John in that bleak air
So am I welcomed richer by these blue scapes Greek
    there
So I will voyage no more from home, may I speak here.

This island is heaven away from the dustblown blood
    of cities
See the curve of bay, watch the straggling flower,
    pretty is
The winged sound of tree, the sparse powdered sky
    when lit is
The night. For beauty has surrounded
These black children, and freed them of homeless
    ditties.

As John to Patmos, among each love-leaping air,
O slave, soldier, worker under red trees sleeping, hear
What I swear now, as John did,
To praise lovelong the living and the brown dead.

QUESTIONS ABOUT THE STORIES & POEMS

Frank Collymore: *Hymn to the Sea* (page 3)

1   Why is the final line of the first stanza repeated at the end of each stanza? In what ways does the poet see the sea as contributing to peoples' lives? to his own particular life?

2   Which words appeal most strongly to your senses? Which images describe the contrasting moods and contributions of the sea most vividly to you?

3   If you, like the poet, live in Barbados or another small island, you too will know the sea well. If you live on a large island, or on the mainland, you may be far from the sea and know it very little. Discuss and write about what the sea means to you.

George Lamming: *Catching Crabs* (page 5)

1   In what ways was catching crabs on the sea-shore different from catching them in the village? Why did Boy Blue and his friends pursue it as a pastime?

2   There are strong contrasts between the feelings that Boy Blue has at different moments in the story. Discuss these and try to explain them. What do you think of his behaviour at the end?

3   This story is specially vivid because of the images, e.g. 'they [i.e. the crabs] were very small and decorous, like cups and saucers which my mother bought and put away'. Look for other images that you think are especially effective and explain why you like them.

4   What do you make of the fisherman's action in rescuing Boy Blue, and his attitude towards him afterwards? Imagine that you are the fisherman telling his wife about the incident that evening.

Dennis Scott: *Bird* (page 10)

1   How does the bird in the sky look to the boy below? Why does he point it out to his friend? What does his friend do and say?

2   How do the boy's vision and feelings change: from the way he sees and feels about the bird at the beginning, to how he sees and feels about it at the end?

3   The first 10 lines of the poem make us really see the bird's flight. How does the poet get this effect?

4   Look at the note about himself and this poem written by Dennis Scott on page 10. In what way were the feelings of the boy in the poem complicated? Have you ever destroyed or killed something and then felt ashamed afterwards? Tell the story and try to bring out your feelings before and after it happened.

Timothy Callender: *An Honest Thief*   (page 11)

1   Who is the 'bad man' living in St Victoria Village? Who is the other 'bad man' who comes to live there? In what ways is each considered 'bad'?

2   What role does Mrs Spencer play in the story? Do you think she should have acted differently at any point?

3   How do Mr Spencer and Bulldog try to frighten or intimidate each other? Find the things that each one says to make himself sound tougher or better than the other.

4   Does the title fit the story? Who is the 'honest thief' and why?

Evan Jones: *Song of the Banana Man*   (page 18)

1   What is the song of the banana man? What are some of the occasions on which he sings it? What makes this a song and not just a poem?

2   Why does the tourist speak to the banana man? Why does he reply? How do you think the tourist would feel and think about the banana man after hearing his song and his story? What do you think the banana man feels about the tourist?

3   What does the banana man himself feel about his occupation? Which particular aspects of the banana man's life and character do you most admire? Have a class discussion.

Clyde Hosein: *Crow*   (page 21)

1   How does Crow make a living in Esperance, his home town? What does he really want to do? How does he set about trying to do it?

2   Why is his attempt to achieve his ambition in Port of Spain so unsuccessful? Who was to blame? In what ways was it successful? What did it lead to? Was his father right in believing that Crow was 'doing very well'?

3   Look again at the passages about Esperance and the Savannah. Try to describe a place you know and how you felt the last time you were there.

4   Compare Crow with the hero of *Calypso Finals* (page 59). In what ways are they alike? In what ways are they different? Which of the two is more successful and content, and why?

Mervyn Morris: *Case-History, Jamaica*   (page 28)

1   Which stages of this man, X's, life are we told about? What are we told about each stage?

2   What is a case-history? In what way do the incidents of each stage of X's life contribute to his being 'a case'?

3   The author's note explains the period in Jamaica at which such a case-history could be found. Could it still be found, in the country where you live?

4   Think of an experience in your own life which changed things for you so that after it you saw everything differently. Try to explain your feelings before and after the incident or experience. If you do not want to write about yourself make up a story, but try to make it very realistic.

Olive Senior: *Ascot*   (page 29)

1   What was Ascot like as a young man? What do you know of Ascot's life after he left home? Discuss the evidence of each stage, and what else may have occurred.

2   'I don't think Papa ever recover from the day that Ascot come back'. Compare Papa's reaction to Ascot's appearance and behaviour on that day with that of Mama and Miss Clemmie. Why were their reactions so different? What do you think of Ascot?

3   In what ways is the language of this story different from that of others in this book? How does it affect the telling of the story? Try re-writing part of the story in a language more similar to standard English, or that of, say, *The Peacocks* or *Supermarket Blues*.

4   Write a further page or two suggesting what happens to Ascot and his wife in the next few years. Start with a phrase like, 'The next time I saw Ascot . . .'. Use the language in which you feel you can tell the story best.

Lorna Goodison: *Song for my Son*   (page 38)

1   There is both hope and fear in this poem. Can you find evidence of each?

2   Which sounds can you hear in the poem? What pictures can you see in it? What feelings does the poem give you?

3   What are the poet's feelings for her son? Which lines suggest them?

4   This is the first of a sequence of poems by Lorna Goodison for her son. Many poems have been written about parents or children. *Either* imagine that you have a child, and write a poem for him/her, *or* write a poem for someone special in your own family.

Namba Roy: *An Heir for the Maroon Chief*   (page 39)

1   Why is Nahne's news of such importance to Tomaso? What is Tomaso afraid has happened to his wife and child when he sees that Nahne is so frightened? Why is Nahne really so distressed?

2   How do Tomaso's questions and Nahne's replies build up tension in the telling of this story? Pick out and discuss each exchange between them.

3   What does Tomaso's behaviour before and after he gets the news tell us about his character? What do think of him as a chief, husband, father? Tell or write about Tomaso, giving reasons to support what you say.

A. L. Hendriks: *An Old Jamaican Woman thinks about the Hereafter*   (page 43)

1   What is 'the hereafter'? What has the old woman heard about it that she would not like? Where has she got her ideas from? What would she like instead?

2   What does she believe she must do in order to achieve her own hope of 'the hereafter'? Which resolution would she find most difficult? How does this add to your picture of the old Jamaican woman?

3   This poem expresses the thoughts of an old woman, living near the sea, in rural Jamaica. Either choose a character from another story or poem in this book, or think of an old person you know. Write a poem or story about her/him, looking back on her/his life and thinking about whatever 'hereafter' she/he believes in.

Samuel Selvon: *The Village Washer*   (page 45)

1   How did Ma Procop set about taking over the village laundry business from Ma Lambee? Were her methods fair? Did Ma Lambee deserve to lose the business?

2   Why does Ma Procop win in the end? Why does Ma Lambee run away terrified? What do you think Ma Procop whispered to her that the villagers couldn't hear? Was there really obeah in the village?

3   Study the characters of Ma Lambee and Ma Procop. In what sense are they both 'bad women'? Compare the way they treat each other with the way the two men treat each other in Timothy Callender's story, *An Honest Thief* (page 11).

4   Imagine that you are the villagers:
— complaining about the way Ma Lambee does the washing
— talking about Ma Procop coming
— talking about the obeah
— talking about Ma Lambee leaving the village
Improvise these scenes. Write one of the scenes as a play-script: you may write it together and base it on your improvisation.

Fred D'Aguiar: *The Day Mama Dot Takes Ill*   (page 52)

1   How does the natural world respond to Mama Dot's illness? List each instance. How does the natural world show that Mama Dot is recovering from her illness? Describe each sign.

2   Do you believe that all these unnatural occurrences could really happen when someone is ill? Why does the poet write about them in relation to Mama Dot's illness?

3   Can you remember an incident in your own life which seemed to make your world turn upside down? Describe it in a poem or a story. The incident could be sad or happy.

F. D. Weller: *The Peacocks*   (page 53)

1   What do you know about the young man's childhood? How has his life changed? Do you think he is happier?

2   What does he remember about the peacocks? Why is it, do you think, that he remembers them when he is lonely and out of work?

3   How does the young man remember Mrs Dawkins? What do you think of her personality as revealed in the story?

4   The story ends quite suddenly. Imagine what happened next, and write the next chapter.

Martin Carter: *Listening to the Land*   (page 58)

1   What experience does the poet describe? (You may find it helpful to read the poet's note about himself on page 141.)

2   Where does he have this experience? What do you know about 'the land' to which he refers? Why might 'some buried slave' there want to speak again?

3   One line, from the first stanza, is repeated in the second and the third stanzas; one from the second is repeated in the third. Which lines are these? Why are they important? How is the poem built around them? Try writing a poem yourself in which you build up lines from earlier stanzas into the last stanza.

Michael Aubertin: *Calypso Finals*   (page 59)

1   At this year's semi-finals, Mighty Mighty is apprehensive from the start. His fears'and suspicions affect his behaviour towards his fellow calypsonians. Pick some examples which show this.

2   What has happened to prevent Mighty from becoming calypso king in previous years? What does he think has caused this?

3   Mighty is convinced that it is obeah that has caused him to fail in this year's finals. What other explanation could you give?

4   Tell or write a story about yourself or someone else who expects to fail at something important. Try to keep the audience or reader interested right up to the end.

Louise Bennett: *South Parade Peddler*   (page 64)

1   What are the different things which the peddler is selling? Who are the different people to whom she is trying to sell them? How does her attitude change towards the people who refuse to buy, and the one who buys?

2   Louise Bennett uses expressive images to describe her customers. For the first one and the second, she uses *similes*:
    'Yuh dah swell like bombin plane fun' (You have swelled up like the fund for victims of a plane bombing) and
    'Yuh soon bus up like Graf Spee' (You will soon bust up like the Graf Spee — a German battleship blown up by its own captain in December 1939 near Montevideo in Uruguay).
For the third and fourth customers, she uses *metaphors*:
    'Yuh no got no use fi it, for yuh
    Dah suffer from hair raid!' (You have no use for it because you have suffered from an h/air raid).

'Dem torpedo yuh teet, sah'.
What do you notice about all four images? You will find a clue in the poet's note about herself, for she says when this poem was written.

3   To enjoy this poem you really have to read it out loud. When you have done so discuss how Louise Bennett makes it so funny, and how she combines everyday speech with rhythm to make poetry.

Hazel Campbell: *Supermarket Blues*   (page 66)

1   Who are the three women shopping at the Three Tees Supermarket? What does each hope to buy there? Who for? How does each cope with the problem of shortages? What else differentiates the three women?

2   Who alone is able to help Miss Maud in her distress? Why can no one else?

3   Which characters did you sympathise with in the story? Why?

4   Imagine you are one of the three women telling the story to a neighbour. Try to write your story in the language and style which the woman would have used.

Agnes Maxwell-Hall: *Jamaica Market*   (page 74)

1   How did Agnes Maxwell-Hall come to write this poem? (See the note she wrote about herself, on page 146.) Which of the things listed in her poem would have been painted on the walls of Falmouth wharf? What else does she list? Where would she have seen them?

2   What has the poet added to the names of things sold at the market? What does this do to them? How has the poet arranged her names and descriptions so that this isn't just a list, it's a poem?

3   Think of a scene or occasion which you know well, at which many colours are on display, e.g. Carnival, a wedding, a market, a bus station. Describe it in prose or poetry, making it as vivid as you can.

Grace Nichols: *Childhood*   (page 75)

1   What aspect of her childhood does Grace Nichols recall in this poem? What is a watershed? Why does she remember her childhood as a watershed?

2   What is the meaning of the poet's reference to Sunday School? Do you believe that fish have souls? What are the consequences for the fish described in this poem? You may like to re–read what Grace Nichols says about this reference in her note on page 147.

3   Discuss each description in the poem. Which do you find specially vivid? Make a list of images that are important to you as memories of your own childhood: try to make them vivid, full of sounds and smells that capture your own feelings. Then organise them into your own poem.

Ralph Prince: *Sharlo's Strange Bargain*   (page 76)

1   What was the bargain which Sharlo made? Why was Sharlo unable to keep it? What happened in consequence?

2   What do you know about Sharlo at the beginning of the story? What changes take place in him: physically, in his way of life, in his character? Why does he change?

3   Write a report for a local newspaper about the strange events in Glentis Village. Try to present it as real 'hard' news.

4   The story of Sharlo's strange bargain is, says Ralph Prince, 'an old, old story, and they say it's true'. Do you know another folk story with a moral? If so, tell or write one, trying to make it as vivid and exciting as this one.

John Robert Lee: *Spring*   (page 84)

1   Whom is the poet addressing? What is he doing? What does the poet hope to learn from him? (You may find it useful to read John Robert Lee's note about himself on page 145.)

2   Why do you think John Robert Lee has set the poem out in this way on the page? What does it add to the poem?

3   Why is *Spring* the title of the poem? What other meaning for the labourer's digging and divining (search) for water is contained in the poem besides the literal one? In what sense do you find this a religious poem?

John Hearne: *Only One Blow of the Wind*   (page 85)

1   Why was the narrator, Andrew, aware of the danger he and his hog-hunting party were in? What did they do for safety? Why did that not protect them to the end? Which members of the party were lost, assumed drowned? How were they saved?

2   Why was Carl in particular so anxious to get back home? What might have happened if, as he wanted, they had gone on? What other evidence is there in the story of experience saving lives? In what ways do the animals sense danger and know what to do?

3   Who are Graham and Ferdie? What part do they play in the story?

4   Which other natural disasters have you heard about? Have you experienced any sort of disaster? If so, tell a story about it. If not, make up a story about a hurricane, drawing on the facts and descriptions in this story.

H. D. Carberry: *Nature*   (page 94)

1   What does the poet say we do not have? What does he say we do have? Is there a correspondence between these things?

2   The poet contrasts four seasons with four days. How does he use his five senses to capture the way the days affected him? Pick out phrases and words with which the poet appeals to our senses. Look especially for the ways he uses the sound of the words to reflect the meaning.

3   Tell or write about the days which you especially remember and which you think are best. Try to think, and then describe, how all your senses are affected by the colours, sounds, smells, tastes and feel of the best days and what you do on them.

Andrew Salkey: *Linda's Bedtime*   (page 95)

1   Why does Linda not want to go to bed? What is her mother's argument, and inducement, to get her there? How does her father follow? Why does Linda pretend not to understand the difference between the words that each tells her?

2   This passage starts with an excellent example of an effective image, combining simile and metaphor. Discuss the image in detail; then find and discuss other good images in this passage.

3   Linda tells her father that she knows the difference between Anancy and the Lord. Do you think that prayers should always be serious or is it possible to have 'belly-laugh and sweet joke' in a prayer?

Neville Dawes: *Acceptance*   (page 98)

1   Each stanza opens with the words 'I praise'. What particular thing does the poet praise in the first three stanzas? To what does all the praise lead the poet in the final stanza? (You will find it helpful to read the note about the author on page 142.)

2   Why do you think the poem is called *Acceptance*? Could it as well be called a hymn of praise? To whom should the hymn be addressed?

3   Which experiences described by the poet seem to you the most vivid? How has he made them so?

Michael Anthony: *Rosalie Gidharee*   (page 100)

1   This passage describes the first two meetings between Shellie, the narrator, and Rosalie Gidharee. What is similar and what is different about their two meetings?

2   What does Shellie feel about his father? What clues are there to his feelings? How does Rosalie react?

3   Where do both meetings between Shellie and Rosalie take place? How is the place described? How do these descriptions add to the mood of the story?

4   Write a story about the first meeting of two young people who take a liking to each other and become friends. Try to place their meeting in a setting which you know well, as Michael Anthony has done.

Edward Kamau Brathwaite: *The Pawpaw*   (page 108)

1   What do you know about the children who brought the pawpaw to the poet? How did they present it?

2   The pawpaw is described first as being like a bomb, then like a nugget of gold. What are such images called? What does the first image tell you about the way in which the pawpaw was carried? What does the second tell you about the way in which the poet saw the pawpaw?

3   Do you own something which is very precious to you, although it may seem worthless to other people? Describe it and how you got it, and explain why it means so much to you.

Roger Mais: *World's End*   (page 109)

1   What do you know about the Old Man's life and his family? Why is the death of his donkey such a tragedy for him? Why is the story called *World's End*?

2   Who are all the people on whom Old Ben feels he must call? What does he tell them? How do they respond? In what way is the response of the final person different from that of all the others?

3   The story starts in the morning and ends at night. How are the stages of the story matched by, or reflected in, the changes in time and weather? In what way do they contribute to the changes in mood of the story?

4   How does Tim's attitude towards his father change during the story? Write a story about someone you thought you knew well, in which you are suddenly able to see him or her differently.

A. J. Seymour: *There Runs a Dream*   (page 115)

1   What does the poet imagine lies buried beneath the rivers of
Guiana? Who built them? Why were they built?

2   Look at a map of Guiana (Guyana) and pick out all the rivers
that flow into the sea. If the rivers could talk, what might they say?

3   What does the poet mean by 'History moved down river'? Again,
a map of Guyana will help you. What remains of earlier times are there
in your country? Write a poem about them.

Earl Lovelace: *George and the Bicycle Pump*   (page 116)

1   How many times in the story does George's bicycle pump
disappear? How does he find out, each time, and what does he think and
feel about it? Why does George persist in buying a new bicycle pump,
and leaving it on the bicycle, each time it disappears?

2   Read again the opening scene of the story. Which details has the
author selected and described? What is their effect?

3   Act out the episode between George and the 'fellar' in the
Savannah. How and why does their relationship change? Discuss the
significance of the episode.

4   George and his wife, Beulah, look at life in very different ways.
What are the main differences between them? What do you think has
made Beulah react as she does? Write another story in which Beulah
appears.

Derek Walcott: *As John to Patmos*   (page 126)

1   With whom does the poet compare himself all through the poem?
From which island, in which sea, does each come? (You may find the
author's note helpful, see page 150.)

2   Which images of Derek Walcott's own island seem to you to be
specially vivid? Discuss and expand them.

3   'This island is heaven away from the dustblown blood of cities.'
What feelings about his island does the poet express?

4   What resolutions does the poet make? Which other poems in the
book lead you to feel that their authors have made similar resolutions?

Notes about the Writers
in alphabetical order

The authors have written about themselves and their work specially for this book — except for those no longer alive, when the note has been written by someone closely related to them.

Michael Anthony
Rosalie Gidharee, p. 100

I turned to writing *Green Days by the River*, my third novel, in order to see if I could feature a landscape that I know and love — a landscape of lush and charming scenery — and at the same time tell a story of young love and innocence, of naivety, and of the pain and pleasures of growing up. The landscape is that of Mayaro, the village in Trinidad which I was born in 1932, and where I went to school. For the story I thought I would use characters who were friends of my youth, people whom I knew closely, and could portray 'in character'.

My other purpose in choosing Mayaro was to tell a story of a remote country village and make that village live. I am not sure whether I have succeeded, but I am sure the exercise gave me a great deal of pleasure, making me draw on many of the experiences of my early life. When I was 22 I travelled to England; after several years there, my family and I went to live in Brazil. In the early 1970s we returned to live in Trinidad.

Michael Aubertin
Calypso Finals p. 59

I was born in Castries, St Lucia, in 1948. I remember entertaining my classmates with adventure stories when I was at school. Later, when I became a teacher, my students enjoyed our story-telling periods the most. I have been writing since I was fifteen. I wrote this story after becoming a calypsonian and performing on stage before large audiences. I am the Independence Calypso King of St Lucia and have recorded many calypsoes. I have also recorded an album of humorous dialect stories called *Mighty Laughs*. I won a BBC Caribbean Magazine competition with *Calypso Finals* in 1977 and it was broadcast by the BBC along with one of my songs. Some of this story is true as I once myself experienced what it was like to 'flop'.

From 1986–7 I did an M. Ed. at Manchester University, and I know that my experiences there will form the basis of many stories in the future. Afterwards I was glad to get back home to my wife and three children in St Lucia. I hope to publish a book of short stories one day soon.

Louise Bennett
South Parade Peddler, p. 64

I wrote this poem more than forty years ago, during World War II. As you see, it is in Jamaican creole. I've been writing in this Jamaican language since my early teens. The first poem of this sort I wrote was based on what I heard people say while travelling in a tram–car. I started to listen to people and I said, Well this is what I should be writing instead of about palm trees dreaming!

My poems start with people, mostly: with something I hear somebody say or something I see somebody do. I was really fascinated by the South Parade peddler – her voice, what she was saying, even her movement; and the rhythm of her speech, the sudden changes between begging and cursing; and the precariousness of it all – she had to look out for police, because what she was doing was illegal.

Edward Kamau Brathwaite
The Pawpaw, p. 108

I wonder why this poem is so popular? Is it because it is true? It 'happened' very much as you read it. I was an Education Officer in Ghana at the time, and was sheltering from the rain on a friend's verandah when I saw the bunch of schoolboys coming towards me with the gift of the pawpaw. Ghana, as you know, was once called 'The Gold Coast', because it was (and is) very rich in that mystic and beautiful mineral. When I was in Ghana, I also wrote several plays for schoolchildren: *Four Plays for Primary Schools* (two for Christmas and two dramatised Anancy stories) and *Odale's Choice*.

I was born and educated in Barbados. In 1949 I won the Barbados Scholarship to Cambridge University in England where I took degrees in History and Education. It was after Cambridge that I worked as an Education Officer in Ghana, from 1955 to 1962. Since then I have taught at the University of the West Indies, Mona, Jamaica, where I am now Professor of Social and Cultural History and publish and edit *Savacou*, the journal of the Caribbean Artists Movement, which with Andrew Salkey and John La Rose, I founded in London in 1966. Since 1967 I have been engaged in writing and publishing a series of long poems: *Rights of Passage, Masks, Islands, Mother Poem, Sun Poem* and *X/Self*. In December 1987, along with George Lamming, I was awarded my country's second highest official award, the Companion of Honour of Barbados (CHB) for contribution to literature.

Timothy Callender
An Honest Thief, p. 11

I was born in the parish of St Michael, Barbados, and educated at Combermere School, the University of the West Indies (where I gained a B. A. in English and a Diploma in Education) and the University of London (where I gained an M. A. in Art and Design in Education). I started writing and painting from the time I was in school, writing of and painting the landscape, people and events I see around me. The late Frank Collymore, editor of *Bim*, took an interest in my work; I wrote also for radio, where he and another great storyteller, Alfred Pragnell, read my work. I have taught English, Art, General Studies, History and other subjects in various Caribbean islands, in secondary schools, colleges and university. At present, I am teaching in Barbados, at a secondary school and at the UWI campus here. I spend the rest of my time creating plays, painting and exhibiting pictures, and writing for various magazines and newspapers and for radio. My stories have been published as a collection, *It So Happen*, and in many anthologies for schools. This story, *An Honest Thief*, is still one of my favourite stories.

Hazel Campbell
Supermarket Blues, p. 66

I have lived in Kingston, Jamaica, all my life. In childhood I was known to be a 'day dreamer'. I had many ideas for stories and an intense love for English language and literature at school. However, I did not have the confidence to attempt writing until I graduated from the University of the West Indies with a degree in English and Spanish. I taught at a high school for a while in the '60s, and during this time I became increasingly frustrated by the almost total absence of published local or Caribbean writing which could be used to stimulate my students' interest in language. This frustration helped to push me into trying my hand at writing. *Supermarket Blues* came out of the era of the '70s in Jamaica, when, as in many other Third World countries, dwindling foreign exchange created problems with the supply of consumer goods, including some basic food items. In addition to showing how the crisis affected three different women, the story makes several points about human relationships. I hope you will spot these.

H. D. Carberry
Nature, p. 94

For almost all my life I have lived surrounded by the sort of nature described in this poem. Although I was born in Montreal, Canada, in 1921, at the age of five I was brought by my West Indian parents to Jamaica; apart from periods abroad for study, I have lived here ever since. I started writing when I was at school and continued for some time after, but since taking up law I have had little time for it. I am now a

Court of Appeal Judge in Jamaica. But I am still interested in writing and also in reading. I collect books of West Indian literature, and books about the West Indies. And I think the most rewarding and important thing that you can learn when you are a child is to like reading: it opens up the world for you. Also, I think you should learn how to swim, how to ride a bicycle, and how to be useful about the house. Perhaps the second most important thing a child can learn is when to say 'no' to his peers.

I am married and have three children, two boys and a girl. I enjoy law and anything that has to do with people and how they live, work and amuse themselves.

Martin Carter
Listening to the Land, p. 58

This poem was first published in 1951, in a volume called *The Hill of Fire Glows Red*, on the eve of a period of bitter conflict and great suffering in the history of what was then the Colony of British Guiana. Our new constitution of 1952, which was to ensure full internal self-government for the first time, was suspended by the British the following year. The British government then moved their troops into our country, and placed in detention many people, including myself, whose political views they considered dangerous. At that time, when this poem was written, it seemed to me important to be aware of my country's history, and to be sensitive to the special features which have shaped that history; and of course awareness is irreversible.

I was born in Georgetown in 1927 and educated at Queen's College. For some years I was a Civil Servant, and from 1959–67, Information Officer for the Booker Group of Companies in Guyana. I was a member of the delegation to the Guyana Constitutional Conference in London in 1965, and of the Guyana Delegation to the 21st and 22nd Meetings of the General Assembly of the United Nations, sometimes leading the Delegation in 1967 as Guyana's Minister of Information. In 1965, too, I represented Guyana at the Commonwealth Poetry Conference in Cardiff, Wales, and again at the Conference on Caribbean Writing in London in 1986.

Frank Collymore
Hymn to the Sea, p. 3

What this poem says is true: I do live on a small island. I was born in Barbados, in 1893, and have spent most of my life there. I taught English at Combermere School for 48 years, and have edited the magazine *Bim* since 1943. So one·way and another I have come across a great many young West Indians who are trying to write. Several of the West Indian writers who have now had books published and are successful and famous had their first stories or poems published in *Bim*. You may sometime spot a new, unknown writer in the latest number of *Bim*, or you may yourselves send us stories or poems to publish in it. Besides editing *Bim* and teaching English, I have written a few short stories and many poems myself. In 1958 I was awarded the O.B.E. My chief form of recreation is acting; I have appeared in many plays, and always enjoy them.

(*This note was prepared by Frank Collymore for the first edition of* The Sun's Eye *in 1968. He died in 1980.*)

Fred D'Aguiar
The Day Mama Dot Takes Ill, p. 52

Imagine a grandmother who never sleeps. When you wake, first thing, she has already baked bread and is busy chopping firewood, fetching water from the standpipe down the road and has put out the first tub of washing to catch the morning sun to make way for a second wash before midday. Imagine, too, a grandmother who is on her feet when everyone is down with measles, chicken pox, fever, mumps, stomach aches, sprains, cuts, insect bites, toothache, headache or any number of ailments; she is busy fetching cures from bushes she goes out to pick and prepare by boiling, crushing, squeezing, even seasoning. Imagine further a grandmother who says it will rain put on a coat before you go out and there isn't a speck of cloud in the sky, yet when you are out it pours, or she says there will be a birth or a death and a child is born or news of a death comes in. She alone can make the goat stand still and be milked; only she knows which eggs are fresh-laid and which are hatching. Imagine finally what becomes of this world, our world, made and ordered by her, the day she of all people takes ill.

I was born in London in 1960. My parents are Guyanese. I grew up in Guyana, mostly in a small village named Airy Hall, returning to London for my secondary and university education. My first book of poems, *Mama Dot* (1985) has a sequence about my grandmother. A second collection, *Airy Hall*, is forthcoming.

Neville Dawes
Acceptance, p. 98

I grew up in a small village, Sturge Town, in the St Ann hills in Jamaica, in the 1930s. Pimento was the main product of the village, and in the summer holidays everybody helped pick pimento. The summers were perfumed with it. Also, every day we saw the sea ten miles away across the red earth, now bauxite land. I went to school at Jamaica College in Kingston, and then studied at Oriel College in Oxford, England. It was when I returned to the village in which I had grown up that I wrote this poem; I had been away from it for fifteen years. There are two references in the poem which I should like to explain. The first is 'King Arthur': that refers to the legend of the Round Table, with which I identified myself completely as a boy. The second is 'Her' in the last stanza; she is no actual person, but the village thought of and spoken of as a person.

(This note was prepared by Neville Dawes for the first edition of The Sun's Eye *in 1968. He died in 1984.)*

Lorna Goodison
Song for my Son, p. 38

I was born and brought up in Kingston, one of a large family. I have six brothers and two sisters. My mother's family came from Harvey River in Hanover. My father was from St Elizabeth. He died when I was in my teens. All my family relationships have deep meaning for me. I have written several poems about my mother and father, and about my grandmother. *Song for my Son* is the first of a sequence of poems about the time when my son, Miles, was newly born. It appears in my second book, *I am becoming my Mother*. My first book is *Tamarind Season*, and my latest book *Heartease*.

I have been writing poems since I was at high school. At first I used to send them to the *Sunday Gleaner* under a different name. After school I studied art, in Kingston and New York. At times I have spent more time painting than writing, and I have worked professionally as both artist and scriptwriter. But since about 1975 I have concentrated more and more on writing poetry. I find writing poetry is very hard work, although sometimes the results can look so simple. I think I have a responsibility as a writer. Poetry is about truth, and I want to chronicle some of it.

John Hearne
Only One Blow of the Wind, p. 85

I was born in Canada, in 1926, but I came to Jamaica when I was a child and grew up and went to school here. In 1943 I joined the Royal Air Force, during the Second World War. Then, when the War was over, I studied at Edinburgh and London Universities. Since then I have been backwards and forwards between England and Jamaica, many times, working as a teacher and a writer. I have published several novels and short stories, and worked widely as a journalist. For many years, I was Resident Tutor in the Extra-Mural Department of the University of the West Indies, when I was able to teach university courses to people who were unable to be full-time students. I have also taught journalism and writing for radio and television to university students. I am now Secretary of the University's Creative Arts Centre.

A. L. Hendriks
An Old Jamaican Woman thinks about the Hereafter, p. 43

I write wherever I can, on 'planes, trains, in bed, in offices, even walking: whenever I think of something I jot it down on the nearest piece of paper, put it in a pocket and work at it from time to time until the

143

piece is finished. This particular poem was caused by my thinking of several elderly ladies I have known: I want the poem to seem kindly and sympathetic to the old woman it describes.

I was born in Kingston, Jamaica, in 1922 and have been writing since I was about nine; I began with stories and plays, and then, when I was about seventeen, I started to write poems. At school — Jamaica College, Kingston, and Ottershaw College, Surrey, England — my favourite subject was English literature. My work now is in various kinds of business and in reading poetry in public. I continue to write verse; I hope to more and more as it gives me great pleasure. I have published seven books of poetry, some short stories, essays, and several stories for children.

Clyde Hosein
Crow, p. 21

Crow is a composite of a man I knew in my Trinidadian home town and of the performers I met several years later as an agency director in Port of Spain. His was a yearning for self-expression and recognition in a society which seldom provided opportunity for the talented. Indeed, all over the island these would-be crooners braved constant ridicule, scorn and even violence.

I went to London in 1960 and returned to Trinidad in 1963 to find that Crow had emigrated to the English Midlands. I lived in Port of Spain until 1973, working with the Industrial Development Corporation, Radio Trinidad, and the Lonsdale-Hands Organization. I also wrote an arts column for the *Trinidad Guardian* and moderated 'Issues and Ideas' and 'Book Talk' on Trinidad and Tobago Television.

In 1977, in Toronto, I began to write the collection *The Killing of Nelson John*. I was setting out to capture the abuse of innocence in colonial society. 'Crow' is one of these stories.

Evan Jones
Song of the Banana Man, p. 18

Song of the Banana man was written as a memory of my childhood and a tribute to my country. For I was born in one of the chief banana-growing parts of Jamaica — Hector's River, Eastern Portland, in 1927. My father was a prominent banana planter there. One of my brothers, Kenneth Jones, was member of the House of Representatives for Eastern Portland, and a Minister in the Jamaican Government. I went to school at Munro College in Jamaica. Since then I have lived in the United States and in England. I have been a relief worker for the United Nations and a teacher, but mostly I have worked as a professional writer: of film and television scripts, and of books for children. I now live in the country, near Bath, England, with my wife and two daughters, and am working on a novel about the West Indies.

144

George Lamming
Catching Crabs, p. 5

As you will guess if you read my novel, *In the Castle of my Skin*, from which this passage is taken, I was born and educated in Barbados. At school I enjoyed languages particularly — and cricket; in fact, I am still very interested in cricket. During the 20 or more years when I lived in Britain, from 1950, I watched most of the important international Test matches. In Britain I worked in a variety of ways connected with writing. My six novels were published during this period, in addition to several short stories and poems. I returned to live and work in the Caribbean in the mid-1970s, and now live once more in Barbados, on the magnificent bay of Bathsheba, on the Atlantic coast. My present work is concerned with the culture of the entire Caribbean region.

John Robert Lee
Spring, p. 84

This poem was born while I was watching my father-in-law working in a garden. I admired his ease among the plants, the way he expertly cleared the soil. I was helped to see more clearly what the search for faith involves. We have to 'dig down' past all of life's circumstances and our own confusions to find truth, faith and peace. Water is a strong religious symbol for cleaning. This search is a very personal one. Nobody else can do it for you.

As for me, I was born in St Lucia in 1948 and have lived there most of my life. I studied literature at the University of the West Indies. I have been a literature teacher, acted and directed theatre, worked with radio and television. My chosen profession now is school librarian. I write poetry, short stories, newspaper articles. I also preach and teach the Bible among Christian groups. I am married and have two daughters.

Earl Lovelace
George and the Bicycle Pump, p. 116

There are two things I have always loved doing: one is reading and the other is playing. When I was young I found that reading can also be useful as somebody who is in a house reading doesn't get disturbed. I still read everything: westerns, novels, detective stories, poems, plays — the lot. I must have been about 21 when I decided to become a writer: it was a choice between that and being an athlete. I have been writing ever since.

George and the Bicycle Pump grew out of another story which I wrote more than 20 years ago, which was published in the Trinidadian magazine *Voices*. That story was also about George and Beulah, and George was completely despondent about life. He wanted to kill himself and kept suggesting different ways of doing it, but Beulah disagreed with every method he proposed. When I looked at the story again I picked up the idea of the bicycle, which was mentioned in the original; but the new story about the pump is much more hopeful.

Roger Mais: *a note by his sister*
World's End, p. 109

Roger Mais was born in Jamaica in 1905 and died in 1955. His early boyhood was spent in Kingston, but when he was about six or seven, our parents moved to Island Head in St Thomas, way up in the Blue Mountains — even to this day the house is accessible only by bridle path, some three miles from the main road. Later we moved to another property in St Thomas, called New Monklands, far more accessible; it was an old stone house, built in the days of slavery. Roger had a varied career: agriculture, horticulture, journalism, photography. At the same time he was a novelist, poet, painter, playwright. And it was his writing and painting that were real and important to him; the other things were stop-gaps. He published two volumes of short stories, three novels, a good many poems. He edited and published his own magazine. His plays were produced and his paintings were exhibited in Jamaica and in London. He read extensively and worked like a fiend. He was argumentative, pugnacious, warm-hearted and generous.

Agnes Maxwell-Hall
Jamaica Market, p. 74

I was born in Jamaica. I grew up in a house which was seven miles from Montego Bay and two thousand feet up in the hills. Half the island lay below us. It seemed to me without doubt the most beautiful spot on earth. It was also a heavenly spot — literally, for my father was an astronomer, and used to let us look through his telescope at all the wonders of the sky. Falmouth was a few miles along the coast. One day I was there and saw on the walls of the wharf the painted names of the produce bought there: honey, pimento, anatto, limes. Their names made poetry. And that is how *Jamaica Market* came to be written.

I went to school in London, Boston and New York. I now work in a College in New York — and still write poetry.

Mervyn Morris
Case-History, Jamaica, p. 28

I was born in Kingston, Jamaica, in 1937, and I have been working for the University of the West Indies (at Mona) since 1966. The poem, *Case-History, Jamaica*, must have been written in the late 1960s or early 1970s when many of us, young people in particular, were learning to identify 'white bias' and to distrust complacent ignorance of Africa. It was a time of developing Black Consciousness, and of talk about Black Power. On walls all over the place, militant slogans appeared. The poem is suggesting why.

146

My shorter poems have been published in two collections: *The Pond* and *Shadowboxing*; my sequence of poems, *On Holy Week*, is published separately.

Grace Nichols
Childhood, p. 75

I guess this poem came from one of my earliest childhood memories of myself standing calf-deep in rippling brown water, lit up by the sun, and watching the shapes of the fish going by underneath. You see I grew up in a small country village along the Guyana coast. The way the fish drifted into our yard was always a mystery to me. That is why I say, 'Strange recurring mysteries', in the poem, because sometimes when we had a flood after heavy rains there would be no fish around and at other times there would be a whole lot moving slowly, as if they'd been stunned and we'd be able to catch them quite easily with baskets. Of course when we went to church we were never told to pray for anything like fish. But as a child I was also moved by the sight of all those helpless fish.

When I'd grown up I trained and worked as a journalist in Georgetown. Then in 1977 I came to Britain, where I make a living as a writer. My published books include several for children, two collections of poems — *i is a long-memoried woman* and *The Fat Black Woman's Poems* — and a novel, *Whole of a Morning Sky*.

Ralph Prince
Sharlo's Strange Bargain, p. 76

I was born in a village called Bolans, in the southern part of Antigua. As in other parts of the island, the old people there often told Anancy and other stories — such as the tale of a headless jumbee that chased a man for miles after telling him the time. These and other similar stories coloured my imagination and cast it in a certain mould. And this mould gradually became West Indian as I travelled and lived in different parts of the Caribbean and heard similar stories. I spent my childhood in Nevis and St Kitts as well as in Antigua; later I lived in St Thomas in the American Virgin Islands, Guyana and Great Britain, finally returning to Antigua.

I am married with three children. With a background of deep interest and hard work in English at school, it was natural for me to take up writing seriously after a time. I did free-lance journalism for several years, during which time I studied and practised short-story writing.

(*This note is based on the one prepared by Ralph Prince for the first edition of* The Sun's Eye *in 1968. He died in 1985.*)

Namba Roy: *a note by his widow*
An Heir for the Maroon Chief, p. 39

Namba Roy, Fellow of the International Institute of Arts and Letters, was a sculptor, painter and writer. All his work draws on the traditions of his people, the tribal, independent community of the Maroons of Accompong, Jamaica. His novel, *Black Albino*, from which this passage comes, is a story about his community in its early days, when, as former slaves of the Spanish, they had fled from the British invaders to the densely forested Cockpit Country.

Born in 1910, Namba Roy spent his early life among the Maroons and learnt the art of carving from his father and his grandfather, who was also the tribal story-teller. He also inherited from them many traditional African subjects and forms, preserved within the family for over 200 years from their life as a tribal community in the Congo. His mother was of Arawak descent. During the Second World War Roy volunteered as a seaman, was torpedoed and eventually arrived in London. There he continued to practise traditional carving, making many beautiful figures. He held exhibitions in London, Paris, Nice, Stockholm. Two of his finest pieces, carved in ivory, are on permanent exhibition in the National Gallery of Jamaica. He died in 1961. His two daughters, Jacqueline and Lucinda, and his son, Tamba, continue the family tradition of writing, painting and storytelling.

Andrew Salkey
Linda's Bedtime, p. 95

Although my parents were Jamaican and I grew up in Jamaica, I was born in Panama, in 1928. We moved to Jamaica two years later. When I was eight I won the All-Island Elocution Contest. At secondary school — St George's College and Munro College — my favourite subjects were English language and literature, Latin, and Biology; and I was an all-round school-boy athlete. In 1952 I came to Britain and studied English literature at London University. Then I worked in London: for a time as a teacher of English and Latin composition, for many years as a freelance broadcaster for the Overseas Services of the BBC. Since 1976, I have been teaching fiction and poetry writing at Hampshire College, in Massachusetts, USA. All this time I have been writing: adult novels — from *A Quality of Violence*, set in Jamaica, from which this passage has been taken — to *Come Home, Malcolm Heartland*, set in London; poetry; and ten books for young readers, from *Hurricane, Earthquake* and *Drought* to *Danny Jones* and *The River that Disappeared*.

Dennis Scott
Bird, p. 10

I was born in Kingston, Jamaica, in 1939. I began writing when I was at Jamaica College, aged twelve; I wrote poems and a blank verse tragedy,

Medea, which was presented at a school prize-giving. It was at about that time that I decided to be a teacher and a writer. And that is just what I have done. After studying English at the University of the West Indies, I taught in Trinidad and Jamaica. Then I studied theatre for a year in Georgia, USA, and Drama in Education for a year in Newcastle upon Tyne, England. For seven years I was Head of the Jamaica School of Drama. At present I am an Associate Professor, teaching Directing at the Yale School of Drama. Four full-length plays of mine have now been produced in the Caribbean and in England, and two books of poems published. *Bird* has its origins in an actual incident recollected from my boyhood. Like most of my writing, it tries to deal with how complicated feelings often are.

Samuel Selvon
The Village Washer, p. 45

When I went to school in Trinidad, where I was born, we didn't have textbooks like this one in those days. It was all English literature, Dickens and Shakespeare, Byron and Keats. I hated Arithmetic and Algebra, but was top of the class most times in English Composition. I didn't complete my education because things were brown and I had to hustle a work. I started to write during the war, while in the West Indian branch of the Royal Naval Reserve, mainly poetry. After the war I worked as a sub-editor on the *Trinidad Guardian*. During this period I wrote many short stories and articles: *The Village Washer* is one of them. Though the story is set in a small village in Trinidad, the atmosphere and the people are very like what you would find in other parts of the Caribbean. The theme of 'obeah' will be familiar to many though it may be called something else outside of Trinidad.

I came to England in 1950 and have been writing professionally since 1954. Most of my books have been published also in America, and some have been translated. One was done in Braille, for blind people. I have also written a number of plays and three books for children, two of them especially for schools in New Zealand, where they wanted to learn something about the Caribbean. After more than 28 years in England I moved with my family to live in Canada, and visit the Caribbean as often as possible to refresh my sources.

Olive Senior
Ascot, p. 29

I had fun writing *Ascot*. Yet the story, though humorous, does have serious intent. It is a celebration of the many people like Ascot that you and I know – those who are not quite straight, who are unscrupulous in search of their goals, yet who are seemingly indestructible because they are 'bare-face', cunning, and – above everything else – charming. No matter what they do, we find it hard to dislike them. I chose the narrator very carefully: an old childhood friend who is bemused by Ascot yet who, we suspect, is not entirely unimpressed. For although Ascot might seem a villain, he is not totally so. I wanted to elicit sympathy and an understanding of the social forces that produce the Ascots of this world and drive them to succeed. For Ascot's climb upwards represents a powerful characteristic of Caribbean peoples – an intense drive to self-improvement, often played out through emigration, often at some cost to both the individual and those left behind.

My own childhood was spent in rural Jamaica. I now live and work in Kingston. The book of short stories in which *Ascot* appears is called *Summer Lightning*. I have also published a collection of poems, *Talking of Trees*.

A. J. Seymour
There Runs a Dream, p. 115

Guyana is where I was born, where I have spent most of my life — and it is the history of Guyana that has inspired most of my writing. I like to read about it and meditate on it. I like, too, to try to find the deep meanings in the life around me. So you will see that the poem in this book is typical of what I write. I can remember quite clearly how I first started to write poetry. One day, in the hot afternoon, I heard music being played on a badly-tuned piano and words began to drop into my unconscious. I heard them fall and liked the sensation and put them down. But that doesn't mean that the words always come to me just right the first time: it took me three hours before I was satisfied with the two opening lines of the sonnet, *There Runs a Dream*.

I grew up in Georgetown and brought up my own family there. After living for a while at Linden and then in Puerto Rico, my wife and I are happily back in our Georgetown home, though our seven children, one adopted, are now grown up and far away.

Derek Walcott
As John to Patmos, p. 126

I have been writing poetry since I was a schoolboy at St Mary's College, Castries, in St Lucia. I was born in Castries in 1930, and lived there until I left for Jamaica on a scholarship to the University of the West Indies. After graduating I taught in Jamaica, St Lucia and Grenada. Then I lived in Trinidad for many years, working as art and literary critic on the *Trinidad Guardian*. Also, I spent a good deal of time with the Theatre Workshop, which I founded in 1959 and directed until 1977. My own plays have been staged not only in Trinidad and all over the Caribbean, but also in North America and Britain. Several have also been published. Many books of my poetry have now been published: from *In a Green Night* in 1962 to *Collected Poems* in 1986.

Although I now spend much of each year teaching at universities in the USA, I am still based in the Caribbean and always regard it as my home: just as when I wrote this poem, *As John to Patmos*. Patmos is a small Greek island, in the Aegean Sea, where St John the Divine was exiled and wrote his 'Book of Revelation', now part of the Bible. My feelings as a young poet about my island of St Lucia, seemed to echo those of St John about the island of Patmos.

F. D. Weller
The Peacocks, p. 53

I'm a Jamaican, and was born in Kingston in 1934, the youngest of five brothers. Before migrating to the USA in 1978, I worked in Kingston, mainly in broadcasting and advertising. I specially enjoyed my work with Radio Jamaica and Rediffusion (RJR) which embraced administration, writing, studio production and presenting my own jazz programme each week. In the USA I have worked as a life insurance salesman. None of these jobs has allowed me much time for writing. The past two decades have indeed been largely devoted to raising a family (four children) and making a living. But I am trying to finish a novel, and hope to find time for more regular writing very soon.

My story *The Peacocks* is based on an actual childhood experience. As a small boy of three or four years old, I was occasionally taken on visits to the home of a wealthy Kingston family of merchants. Wandering through the lavish gardens was a handful of peacocks. As a child I found them awesome, beautiful creatures, though their sound frightened me, and I remember running inside to my father. He insisted on accompanying me back into the gardens to look at the peacocks more closely, and did his best to make me lose my fear of them. In the story the rather troubled, lonely young man revisits the haunt of the peacocks, hoping somehow to recapture not only the sense of wonder, but also the feeling of security which he enjoyed as a child.

Acknowledgements

We are grateful to the following for permission to reproduce copyright material:

The Author, Michael Anthony for an extract 'Rosalie Gidharee' from *Green Days by the River* pp 31–9, (Andre Deutsch Ltd) 1967; the Author, Michael Aubertin for his short story 'Calypso Finals', © Michael Aubertin 1977; the Author, Fred D'Aguiar & Chatto & Windus Ltd for his poem 'The Day Mama Dot Takes Ill' from *Mama Dot* 1985; the Author, Edward Kamau Brathwaite for his poem 'The Pawpaw' from BIM No 27, July–Dec. 1958, p 140; the Author, Timothy Callender for his short story 'An Honest Thief' from *New World* Vol III, Nos 1 & 2 1966/7; the Author, Hazel D. Campbell for her short story 'Supermarket Blues' from *Woman's Tongue: Stories by Hazel D. Campbell*, pp 59–67, (SAVACOU Cooperative) 1985; the Author, Martin Carter for his poem 'Listening to the Land' from *Poems of Succession*, (New Beacon Books) 1977; Ellice Collymore for the poem 'Hymn to the Sea' by Frank Collymore from *Collected Poems: Frank A. Collymore* (Advocate Co.) 1959; Sophie Dawes for the poem 'Acceptance' by Neville Dawes from *Focus* 1956 ed. Edna Manley; Farrar, Strauss & Giroux Inc for the poem 'As John to Patmos' by Derek Walcott from *In a Green Night* (Jonathan Cape Ltd) 1962 © Derek Walcott; the Author, Lorna Goodison for her poem 'Song for my Son' from *I Am Becoming My Mother* (New Beacon Books) 1986; the Author, A. L. Hendriks for his poem 'An Old Jamaican Woman thinks about the Hereafter' from *Focus* 1960 ed. Edna Manley, p 22; John Hearne's Agent for an extract 'Only One Blow of the Wind' from *The Faces of Love* pp 178–189, (Faber) 1957; the Author, Clyde Hosein for his short story 'Crow' from *The Killing of Nelson John*, (London Magazine Editions), 1980 © Clyde Hosein; the Author, Evan Jones for his poem 'Song of the Banana Man' from *Focus* 1956 ed. Edna Manley; the Author, George Lamming for an extract 'Catching Crabs' from *In the Castle of my Skin*, pp 149–153, (Longman) 1970; the Author, John Robert Lee for his poem 'Spring' from *The Prodigal*, (Private) 1983; Longman Group UK Ltd for short story 'World's End' by Roger Mais from *Listen the Wind and Other Stories*, 1986, © Jessie Taylor, and the short story 'Ascot' by Olive Senior from *Summer Lightning and Other Stories*, 1986; Earl Lovelace's Agent for the short story 'George and the Bicycle Pump' from *A Brief Conversion and Other Stories*, (Heinemann Edl. Books) 1988; the Author, Mervyn Morris for his poem 'Case-History, Jamaica' from *The Pond*, (New Beacon Books) 1973; the Author, Grace Nichols for her poem 'Childhood' from *The Fat Black Woman's Poems*, (Virago) 1984; Glenda Prince for the short story 'Sharlo's Strange Bargain' by Ralph Prince from BIM Vol 8, No 30 (1960); Yvonne Roy for the extract 'An Heir for the Maroon Chief' by Namba Roy from *Black Albino* pp 27–30, (Longman) 1980; the Author, Andrew Salkey for an extract 'Linda's Bedtime' from *The Quality of Violence* pp 10–12, (New Authors) 1959; Sangster's Bookstores Ltd for poem 'South Parade Peddler' by Louise Bennett from *Louise Bennett: Selected Poems* pp 63–4, ed. Mervyn Morris 1983 corrected R/P; the Author, Dennis Scott for his poem 'Bird' from *Young Commonwealth Poets '65*, ed. P. L. Brent, West Indian Section, ed. Andrew Salkey (Heinemann) 1965; the Author, Samuel Selvon for his short story 'The Village Washer' from *Ways of Sunlight*, (McGibbon & Kee) 1957, (Longman) 1973; the Author, A. J. Seymour for his poem 'There Runs a Dream' from KYK-OVER-AL, Vol 6, No 19; the Author, F. D. Weller for his short story 'The Peacocks' from *Focus*, 1956 ed. Edna Manley (Extra Mural Dept. UCWI) pp 50–4.

We have unfortunately not been able to trace the copyright holder of 'Jamaica Market' by Agnes Maxwell Hall and would appreciate any information which would enable us to do so.